PARANORMAL

Also by Raymond Moody

Glimpses of Eternity (with Paul Perry)

Life After Loss

Life After Life

The Last Laugh

Reunions (with Paul Perry)

Coming Back (with Paul Perry)

The Light Beyond (with Paul Perry)

Reflections on Life After Life

PARANORMAL

*My Life in Pursuit
of the Afterlife*

RAYMOND MOODY, MD

with Paul Perry

HarperOne
An Imprint of HarperCollinsPublishers

HarperOne

HarperCollins books may be purchased for educational, business, or sales promotional use. For information please write: Special Markets Department, HarperCollins Publishers, 10 East 53rd Street, New York, NY 10022.

HarperCollins website: http://www.harpercollins.com

HarperCollins®, 📖 ®, and HarperOne™ are trademarks of HarperCollins Publishers.

FIRST EDITION

Library of Congress Cataloging-in-Publication Data
Moody, Raymond A.
    Paranormal : my life in pursuit of the afterlife / Raymond Moody with Paul Perry.
        p.   cm.
    ISBN 978-0-06-204642-0
    1. Moody, Raymond A. 2. Near-death experiences—Research. 3. Future life—Research. 4. Parapsychology—Research. I. Perry, Paul. II. Title.
BF1045.N4M665 2010
133.901'3092—dc23
[B]2011025943

12 13 14 15 16 RRD(H) 10 9 8 7 6 5 4 3 2 1

With love to my family
—Raymond Moody

INTRODUCTION

⁓

I have stumbled onto many things in my life, and through this brief loss of stride I have found the world that I live in. It was through a student in my philosophy class who began to question me deeply about his own experience of almost dying that I studied and named the phenomenon known as the near-death experience. Had I not allowed the student to dominate my time with his story, I might have never examined near-death experiences, a path of discovery that led me to write *Life After Life* and led to my lifelong exploration of matters related to the afterlife.

Had I not, literally, stumbled into a bookshelf and been hit on the head by an old book of research by Northcote Thomas, I would not have begun researching the fascinating world of facilitated visions. It is through this line of research that I have been able to re-create many aspects of the near-death experience in patients without them having to almost die. Better yet, I have been able to ease the grief of losing a loved one by helping people to see and otherwise interact with their dead relatives.

And then there are past-life regressions. I tripped into that field of endeavor after listening to a patient who'd gone back in time while engaging in an ordinary session of hypnotherapy.

These are all fields of endeavor that I have gratefully stumbled into. And yes, I believe Mark Twain when he said, "Accident is the name of the greatest of all inventors."

Sometimes, though, I have just stumbled. And the worst of these stumbles have been the result of a disease that clouded everything for me, from my physical senses to my sense of humor to my sense of the world around me. From my late twenties until now, I have lived with a disease called myxedema. This is a difficult affliction to diagnose. Simply stated, with this disease the thyroid gland does not produce enough thyroxine, a hormone that acts in our body something like the volume dial on a radio. The result of this disease is a variety of peculiar symptoms that can lead to myxedema madness, in which the afflicted person gradually loses his mind.

Although myxedema seems as though it should be an easy disease to diagnose, it isn't. Residual thyroid in the bloodstream can trick test instruments into "false positive" readings, which make thyroid levels seem normal when they are not. As a result, my thyroid levels have been erratic over the years, and at times nonexistent. These have been the times when I stumbled the most. At times when my thyroid levels have been low, I have made major mistakes in judgment: given control of my financial life to people I shouldn't have; found myself in mental hospitals; worn thick woolen coats in the middle of a Georgia summer because I was terribly cold; locked myself in my house and refused to come out because I thought the world was against me. I could go on and on.

Over the years I have kept this condition quiet—or as quiet as I possibly could—thinking that it might affect the perception of me or my work. But now I have become wiser about my illness and its effects on my persona. Instead of working against me, it has made me more empathic and understanding of those who are faced with end-of-life issues. It has also made me look at illness as an altered state that changes our perceptions of ourselves and the world around us as much as, say, an out-of-body experience or even a near-death experience. Like those and other altered states, illness can make us feel both weak and powerful at the same time, depending upon our level of acceptance of the way things are and our ability to dig deep and find new sources of strength. When one man said to me—as others have said—that his near-death experience drained him of strength yet filled him with hope, I understood completely how that could take place. I also understand that to accept such a contradiction, one often has to experience an altered state as powerful as illness.

That's why I feel it's important to begin this book by recounting the battle of my own life. Without such a near-fatal illness, I wouldn't have the empathy for others necessary to continue my research in the field of the afterlife. And without it, I wouldn't have had my own near-death experience, an event that taught me more in a few minutes than years of research and lecturing.

So what I am trying to say, dear reader, is that if the presentation of my attempted suicide makes you doubt my work or the value of its lessons, you should stop reading now. Let me just say that I think this experience has made me more honest about myself and my work; without it, I would lack that dimension that is not present in many doctors, the one that goes beyond knowledge and into the realm of actually being a patient. To paraphrase

William Osler, the father of modern surgery, *a man who has been a patient becomes a much better physician.*

That has certainly been the case with me.

My switch from physician to patient came in January 1991. This was before my myxedema had been properly diagnosed. My thyroid level had dipped off the charts, although I didn't know it. I just knew that I had not felt well for months, but somehow I had convinced myself that it was world events combined with the impact of those events on my personal situation that was making me ill.

This was the year that Iraqi ruler Saddam Hussein decided to attack Kuwait for stealing his country's oil. It was also the time when a new book of mine was being published. *Coming Back* was a study of past-life regressions that I had worked on for years. I had made some astounding discoveries in this work. I had found ways in which modern medicine could use these hypnotic transitions into the past to help patients overcome long-standing psychiatric problems. I had also discovered that a large number of patients seemed truly to go back in time to past lives. Not only did they *say* they had, but many of them provided proof through their hypnotic regressions that they had indeed lived in an earlier era. I had collected this proof from the patients during my sessions with them. I had established to my satisfaction that if they hadn't actually lived in the past, they had somehow been channeled very vivid information linking them with the past.

I was very excited about this book. Not only could it change the lives of many patients with long-standing psychiatric problems, but it would open another door into my continuing study of life after death.

But as the summer progressed, it became more and more obvious that the publication of my book and world events were about to collide. Saddam Hussein was preparing his attack on Kuwait, and our president was lining up international support for an attack on Saddam. These events couldn't have converged at a worse time for me. My marriage had fallen apart, I had been defrauded out of a fortune and had little money left, and I was exhausted from an imbalance of thyroid in my system, a condition that wasn't diagnosed yet. I begged my publisher to delay the book tour until the coming "mother of all battles" (as Saddam called it) was over. "If I go out on tour now, I'll be canceled in every state," I told the publisher. "I don't think people want to hear about my work when a war is starting."

Surprisingly, no one at the publishing house seemed to understand what I was talking about. Instead, they launched the press tour two days before Saddam's troops rolled into Kuwait.

My first stop was New York City. I was ill by the time I reached the Big Apple from Georgia, but still ready to tell the world about the findings in my new book. But there was no need to be ready. All of my media appearances were canceled as Iraqi tanks rolled into Kuwait. "Of course," I said as a TV producer told me she didn't have an extra reporter to do an interview with me. "Why would you? For once, present life is more exciting than past lives."

I visited each of several media outlets on my schedule and got the same comment from each of them: Operation Desert Storm was the biggest thing going. They couldn't waste a minute on any other coverage. "We're hardly covering the Yankees," said one distressed producer.

I left New York the next day for Boston, where no one would interview me either. "Go home," said a blunt-spoken producer. "Saddam's getting everything we've got." After a day in old Beantown I was interviewed by exactly no one. I was zero for eight: no press interviews and eight studio visits.

I pressed on. By the time I left Canada I was zero for twelve. Well, sort of. One Canadian station found a few minutes to interview me and said they would run the interview at a later date. I don't know if the interview ever ran. I didn't care. I was getting sicker.

By the time I reached Denver I knew I should see a doctor about my rapidly declining thyroid level. There I could get a blood test and be prescribed an appropriate amount of thyroid medication to get my blood level back where it should have been. But I didn't see a doctor. The lack of thyroid had clouded my cognition so much that I thought the haze I was living in was due to severe depression I felt from being on the road and pushing a dead book, one that had been killed by world events.

And so I pressed on, one for eighteen by the time I left Denver.

California was next. By the time I landed in Los Angeles I was seeing the world in black and white, a danger sign for me of very severe thyroid deficiency. I was accustomed to the routine by now. A public relations person would pick me up at the airport and then tell me how many of the planned interviews for that day had been canceled. Then we would drive to the ones that hadn't been canceled, only to find that they had been too busy the past week to remember to cancel by phone. A couple of the stations did hurried interviews out of courtesy, and by the end of the day I was on another airplane headed for San Diego.

It was in San Diego that the idea to kill myself took hold. I sat in my hotel room, looking down at the street below, and considered prying the window open and taking a final leap. Every day it was feeling as though tomorrow would be the day everything came apart. Being a psychiatrist, I knew that *presque vu* was the name for that feeling. It means a constant state of frustration. Now, alone in this San Diego hotel room at the end of a failed press tour, I was ready to end the despair once and for all.

I called Paul Perry, my co-author, in Arizona. We had been talking daily as my tour progressed across the country, and he knew how down and depressed I had become. But the conversation we had from San Diego alarmed him. I shared with him my latest plan. I was going to figure out a way to open the window—hotel windows rarely open all the way just for this reason—and throw myself into the alley below.

Paul had a different plan. "We can always do another press tour," he said.

It was worse than that, I said. I had been watching my life unravel for some time, and now it was finally happening. I could see it coming apart right before me, like springs and screws coming out of the back of a wristwatch. That was it. My life was broken. I wanted out.

I spoke to Paul for more than an hour and then, exhausted, fell asleep. In the morning I left for Atlanta.

I hoped things might improve when I returned to the comfort of home, but they didn't. I could hear tension in my own voice as I explained to my friends what a failure the lengthy press tour had been. I am exhausted, I said to my friends, who looked genuinely concerned. I made an appointment to see my doctor on Monday, but by Sunday I was completely over the edge, deep in the grip of myxedema madness. With a large bottle of the painkiller Darvon in my possession, I got in my car and drove to my office at the university. There, I reasoned, I would lock the door and take an overdose of painkillers sufficient to kill me.

In my office I opened the bottle of Darvon and poured them out onto my desk. Then I began to take them several at a time with gulps from a can of Coca-Cola. I took about two dozen of the pills and then sat down at the desk. For some reason I called my co-author Paul.

"I've done it," I said with a note of finality.

"Done what?" he asked.

"I've taken pills and I'm dying," I said.

I could hear the controlled panic in Paul's voice as he started to ask a series of questions: "What did you take? How many did you take? Where are you?"

I became somewhat angry at the line of questioning. I could tell that he wanted to get enough information to somehow intervene from Arizona. But I didn't want an intervention. What I wanted was good conversation in the final moments of my life.

"Look, Paul, I have researched death and I know it's nothing to be afraid of. I will be better off dead."

And that was genuinely how I felt. Myxedema madness had put me in the throes of a paranoia and despair so great that I felt everyone would be better off if I was no longer around. No amount of talk could convince me otherwise. Paul suggested a number of possible solutions to my problems, including an agent and CPA to straighten out my money problems and a new press tour to arouse interest in the book. I would hear none of it. I was ready to die.

"You know, Paul, being alive holds more fear for me than being dead. I have talked to hundreds of people who have crossed into death, and they all tell me that it's great over there," I said. "Every day I wake up afraid of the day. I don't want that anymore."

"What about your children?" Paul asked.

"They'll all understand," I said resolutely. "They know I'm not happy here. They'll be sad, but they'll understand. It's time for me to leave."

I could hear someone jiggling the office door knob as we spoke. Then there was a pounding on the heavy wooden door, a couple of raps at first and then a persistent drumbeat. Then a loud voice. "Campus police, open the door."

I ignored the demand and kept talking to Paul, taking a few more pills as we spoke. Within seconds a key was slipped into the door lock and the door sprang open. Policemen rushed in, and before I could say much of anything they had put my hands behind me and sat me on the floor.

One of the policemen picked up the phone and began talking to Paul. Apparently Paul asked about the presence of pills, because the policeman began to count the pills on the desk. When he was done, he dropped the phone on the desk and from his police radio dialed 911.

An overdose of Darvon has little effect on a person until it reaches a certain blood level. Then the painkiller overwhelms the heart's beating mechanism and quickly stops it cold. A dentist friend who had seen someone overdose on Darvon said it was like falling off a table. The person was going along fine until they just dropped. I knew that the same thing would happen to me shortly. All I had to do was wait. I sat patiently on the floor as emergency medical technicians charged up the stairs with their gurney and equipment.

"Are you okay?" asked one of the EMTs.

"Sure," I said, and I was. Never better, actually. I was not afraid of death, but I had obviously become very afraid of life.

Things began to happen very fast after that. My chest felt very heavy, and I had the feeling of slipping into a dark blue place. They hoisted me onto the gurney and strapped me in and rolled me quickly down the passageway to the waiting ambulance.

As they loaded me into the ambulance the world around me began to fade. The concerned EMT was in my face, trying to keep me awake. Another EMT was drawing something into a very large syringe, probably adrenaline, to inject into my heart. "Better get going," shouted one of the policemen as he slammed the rear doors. I could feel the ambulance accelerate, hitting speed bumps hard as we headed for the hospital. An elephant was sitting on my chest. My eyes were closed, or at least I think they were. Either way, I could see nothing.

After decades of studying the process of death, I knew what was most likely coming next. I would have the feeling of moving rapidly through a tunnel; maybe I would see my grandmothers and grandfathers. Certainly I would have a life review before it was all over. I hoped that would happen. As far as I was concerned, my best years were behind me. If anything excited me it was the past.

Now I could relive it again. . . .

CHAPTER ONE

I was born on June 30, 1944, the very day my father shipped out for World War II. I don't know what my mother thought as she labored to give birth to me that summer day. Given the way her life had gone up to that point, she probably thought that her husband would be killed in the war and would never see his newborn son. Already in her young life, eight of her fifteen brothers and sisters had died in childhood, and one more would be lost in the war. Death had been a constant companion for Mom, and it would be safe to say that she didn't expect a better future.

I know mine was a difficult birth. Mom was young, I was large, and negative thoughts about Raymond Sr.'s likelihood of returning from war were on her mind as she struggled with my childbirth.

Childbirth, dark memories, and fear of the future all added up to a tremendous case of depression that my young mother would only talk about with her parents. In those days people didn't talk freely about their emotions, as they do now. Americans were almost devoutly stoic, expected to show endurance in the face of adversity rather than let anyone know how they truly felt. The result for my mother was a worsening case of depression, which she had to hold inside rather than express.

I think the town of Porterdale, Georgia, was filled with women coping with the same level of depression as my mother. World War II had emptied the town of all its young men, and the women of Porterdale lived with a daily uncertainty about whether their sons, husbands, and lovers would come home alive.

The war also left them childless. Few children had been born since the war started in 1941. And now, with my birth in 1944, an event of some importance had occurred in the town of Porterdale. The town had a baby.

That was good for my mother. When she needed a rest or just some time alone to deal with her depression, Grandmother and Grandfather Waddleton would take over the role of parenting. They doted over me like I was the only child they had ever seen, passing me constantly from one to the other in an effort to give my mother breathing space. It was through them that I was "shared out" to the rest of the community, an arrangement that gave me a large and caring family.

All of the women in the neighborhood who were about the age of my grandmother unofficially adopted me as a grandchild of their own. Two doors down was Mrs. Crowell. She became one of the most important figures in my life. I remember her as being a sweet but very strong woman, the kind I would eventually be the most happy with in marriage. I would go to see her all the time—as an infant and later as a preteen. She allowed me to come in without even knocking, which I did frequently. Once inside, I would curl up on her sofa and dream. She was among the most encouraging people in my life. Her son told me at her funeral years later that she would hold me on her lap and repeat over and over to me, "Raymond, you are going to be a very special person someday."

Next to us was the home of Mrs. Day, who baked and cooked all the time and let me sample with impunity anything that came out of the oven. Best of all were her chocolate chip cookies, followed by puffy home-baked white bread.

Then there was Grandmother Moody, my father's mother. She lived about a mile away. I spent many hours there, smothered with kisses and given great praise for looking just like my father, who was at that time struggling with the daily dangers of combat in the Pacific Theater. I don't think she expected to see him alive again, and sometimes she hugged me just a little too hard.

Mrs. Gileaf, Mrs. Martin, Mrs. Ally—to all of these women I was a novelty because I was a baby. I remember well being held, rolled around in a stroller, or rocked by each of these beautiful people. They were the ones who made my childhood such a big and bright place in my mind.

Porterdale was on the wide and fast-flowing Yellow River, which powered a sawmill. The streets were tree-lined, the sidewalks were clean and new, and the atmosphere was bucolic. Porterdale was the perfect little town. The most memorable place of all, though, was the front porch. Believe me, in Porterdale in the forties there was nothing to do but sit on the porch and talk. That is what people did. Town folks would stroll the streets at night, going from one porch to the next, trading stories of the war or local news.

It was on the porch one night that I was first introduced to the concept of the return from death. It was in a story that my uncle

Fairley told about his dog Friskie. One day, as the story went, little Friskie got hit and killed by a passing truck. Uncle Fairley was heartbroken as he loaded Friskie into his truck and took the poor little dog to the dump. (Sorry, readers, but that is what we did with dead dogs in Porterdale.) Several days later, an unnerving thing happened: Friskie trotted up the street and showed up on the porch, his tail wagging and his face a vision of happiness. Everyone was moved deeply by the return of Friskie, as was I. Friskie was my protector, and to have him back was a great delight.

I was very young when this event happened, but members of my family spoke about it constantly over the years, especially my aunt May, who found in it powerful religious overtones and alluded to Friskie and the resurrection of Christ all in the same breath. It was this memory of Friskie's return from the dead—implanted by my own family's lore—that led me to be fascinated by near-death experiences later in my life.

If I was the town's baby, I was also the apple of my Grandfather Waddleton's eye. Frankly, no one expected my father to return from fighting the Japanese in the Pacific. Everyone had seen the newsreel footage at the Porterdale Cinema and been shocked at the savagery and brutality happening on islands they had never heard of. Because as far as anyone knew I might already be fatherless, Grandfather Waddleton insisted that I call him "Daddy." That is what my mother told me. She said that it would keep me from feeling fatherless in case my real father didn't return. I knew no difference. I didn't really understand the concept of fatherhood at that point, and Grandfather Waddleton would certainly have been my choice of a father if I'd had such a choice.

I can still see his deep blue eyes and bright smile as he held me close and read to me. Sometimes he would drive me around town in his Model T car, the wind blowing through my wispy hair.

I can remember the feeling of the wind and know from photos that I was squinting from the glare of the sun. It feels good to look at those photos now, which is why I think I was feeling good at the time, riding in a jet-black Model T with the man I thought was my father.

Years later my real father told the story of being on a remote island air base in the Pacific when all the men were told to come to the flight line. They stood there until a silver B-24 touched down with a squeal and revved its way to the hangar where they all waited.

The name of the plane was *Enola Gay*, and the pilot, a small slim man with a puzzled look, had the name tag "Tibbetts" sewn to his flight-suit pocket. A number of civilians and high-level military officers were standing by, and when Tibbetts approached them, a brief speech was made and he was immediately awarded the Distinguished Flying Cross.

My real father's vocabulary expanded that day. He heard the words "atomic bomb" and went away wondering just what such a device was and why the military was making such a big deal out of dropping only one.

Back home, the people of Porterdale were also figuring out what an atomic bomb was. Pictures in the paper showed a mushroom cloud and cities fried right off the map by this new invention. Whatever the atomic bomb was, they welcomed it because it brought the end to a brutal war.

I am told that there was jubilation in the streets and tears of joy. Everyone had expected that an end to the war would come only after a costly invasion of Japan. By some estimates, 500,000

American lives would have been lost in such an invasion, along with the deaths of millions of Japanese, truly the mother of all battles. But this atomic bomb had stopped the war in its tracks. The people of Porterdale were elated.

My mother started reading the newspaper avidly now. Soldiers didn't know when they were coming home, but they did know the number of the ship they would be on. My father sent that number in a letter to my mother, and now she would scan columns of type looking for the ship that would carry my father to California, where he would be transferred to a train to Georgia.

I remember vividly the day we went to Atlanta to pick up my father. We all piled into Grandfather Waddleton's Model T and drove the sixty miles to the train station. The place was chaotic, with families milling around nervously waiting for the trains to arrive. Finally a long troop train pulled into the station, and the crowd pressed in, nearly spilling over the platform.

My mother searched frantically for her husband, and when she saw him she pushed her way through the crowd and flung herself on his chest. I was right behind her, held in the arms of my grandfather. I remember to this day a panicked feeling as my grandfather handed me off to my rightful dad. He pressed me into my father's scratchy woolen coat, and my dad held me tight and close until I began to cry and push away. Dad held me tighter, and as he did the woolen coat felt even rougher on my infant skin. I squirmed and cried, and as I pushed away harder my father held me tighter until I could barely catch my breath.

With my free arm, I reached to my grandfather, and when he didn't reach back I twisted around and held my arms out to my mother, who snatched me away from this intimate stranger.

"It's going to take him a while to get used to you," she said to her husband. "He doesn't quite know what's going on yet."

And she was right. Even at such a truly tender age, I knew a lot was going to change.

Looking back, I can visualize this entire scene from my father's perspective. As a medic in the Army, he had seen some of the most god-awful injuries that modern warfare could dish up. All the while, in what little spare time he had, Dad was dreaming of a homecoming in which he would be reunited with a loving family in Georgia and be able to get on with his life.

And what was the first thing to greet him? A child who was spoiled by the entire town and didn't want to be hugged by a father he had never seen.

Now I can look back and cringe at my behavior. At the time, though, I felt very displaced. I had been the center of my family's universe. Now I was being supplanted by a man I was suppose to call "Dad."

Frankly I had difficulty with this new dad. The man I had been raised to call Daddy, my Grandfather Waddleton, was a smiling and kindhearted gentleman who paid careful attention to me. My new dad proved to be very difficult. He had been a military officer and as a result had developed a sort of crew-cut military bearing that would become his trademark for his entire life. Plus, he would eventually become a surgeon, a personality type that is usually rigid, uptight, and wanting to be in charge of almost every situation. I frequently heard stories in my teenage years about my father yelling in the operating room at nurses or other support staff. I wasn't embarrassed when I heard nurses swear about my father. Rather, I could sympathize with them because I too was frequently on the receiving end of such anger.

One example that sticks in my mind came only months after my father had returned from the war. He was outside my grandparents' house planting some peach trees when I ran into one of the tiny trees with a tricycle and snapped the trunk. It was an accident, and no big deal since there were plenty more saplings where that one came from. Still, my father flew into a rage, yelling at me with such vehemence that I began to cry at the anger that boiled over. And then the yelling continued, until my grandmother came outside and rescued me from the unwarranted tirade.

These angry outbursts took place frequently and were disturbing for everyone who witnessed them. My mother tried to dismiss them by laughing them off, but nobody found them forgivable. I remember after one of his outbursts, my Grandfather Waddleton became very pensive. After a consultation with my grandmother, he went outside and with great animation began to talk to my father. I couldn't see my grandfather's face because his back was to me, but I could see my father's and knew he was hearing something that he didn't like. His jaw was clenching and his face was turning red as his eyes narrowed their gaze on my grandfather.

I couldn't hear what the two men were saying, and it probably would have meant little to me if I had. For me the tone of their voices told the tale of dueling styles, a sharp battle between a gentle man supporting his grandson and a gruff, newly returned veteran who would never admit he knew little about dealing with children.

When the two men stopped talking, with no clear agreement, my grandfather turned and walked back toward the porch. That was when I could see how much the conversation about "tough" versus "love" had taken out of my grandfather. He looked withered as he crossed the lawn, and when he reached the porch he scooped me up and took me inside, his arms trembling as he set me down in the living room and then fell onto the sofa. Grandmother brought him a drink of water, and we sat in silence for a long time.

That was the first of many confrontations between my father and grandfather, and the fact that we all lived together in one house didn't make things easier. My father's years of military training prevented him from backing down. His way of getting what he wanted was yelling and intimidation, attributes that might have worked well in combat but weren't very effective with a two-year-old child. And Grandfather Waddleton wouldn't back down either. He had always been a gentle man, and he wouldn't allow quick anger or gruffness to become the new environment in his home. Since we lived with my grandparents until my father could get into medical school, we all had to live by their rules. But the standoff between my father and grandfather created a lot of unhealthy tension in the family.

I remember once when my father was studying in the living room and I was playing with some toy soldiers not far away. I was standing them up in a line and knocking them over one by one with my index finger. Suddenly, with no warning, my father began to swear loudly. I thought he had slammed his finger in a book, but when I looked at him I could see that the swearing was directed at me.

"Can someone get this kid out of here!" he barked. "I don't need the noise. I'm trying to study!"

He slammed his book down on the wooden floor and stood up. Without saying a word, my grandmother swept through the room, picked me up, and took me outside to be with my grandfather.

I am sure my father and grandfather had words about the incident later, because I saw them talking in the kitchen and could tell that both of them were uncomfortable with the conversation.

Still, it was a conversation between them that was repeated many times before I was four years old. And it was the type of conversation that wore heavily on my grandfather, who never anticipated that the return of my father from the war would bring such tension and anger into his household.

Gradually, my grandparents began to shield me from my father, acting as a protective wall from his anger. They were sympathetic in knowing that he had been changed by the horrible traumas of the war. But they were also afraid that he would traumatize me. Because of that, they made a conscious decision to become the buffer between the two of us.

This buffer wasn't a bad thing, at least not in the beginning. I heard and saw a lot that I wouldn't have experienced had they not taken such a great interest in me. Even though I was so young, they truly fueled the fires of thought for me.

One day, for example, an elderly man died across the street from my aunt's house. Rather than conceal death from me (as so many people do with children), my grandmother walked me down the street and into the house, where she paid her respects to the man's wife. As she did so, I wandered into the family room and discovered the deceased man laid out on a couch.

The sallow look of his skin and the angle of repose of his head showed me the distinct difference between the appearance of death and the appearance of sleep. Even at the age of four, I could tell that this man was dead, although I touched his cold chest with my hands just to make certain.

"Dead people look different, don't they," said my grandmother, coming up behind me. "It's like something has left them and gone somewhere else. Must be the soul."

This may have been the first time I ever heard the word "soul," and it was certainly the first time I thought of anything "leaving the body" upon death. I didn't think of the concept of "soul survival" as being religious in nature, since we never went to church anyway. But I do remember that the idea conflicted with what I assumed happened at death—a complete wipeout of consciousness.

CHAPTER TWO

⌒

I know it sounds ridiculous to think that a four-year-old might have a philosophy about death, but I did. It was a philosophy that was originally formed by all the talk of death that revolved around World War II. Most of the soldiers who died in that horrible war didn't come home. They were either buried in foreign graveyards or totally decimated. The ones who did come home were sealed in a box and were never seen again.

The notion that something might survive bodily death was not something I even thought about. The dead were simply gone.

This was not such a pleasant thought to me as a child, because I always felt that I was going to die. That belief was also a holdover from World War II, where a sense of doom pervaded each and every day. It seemed as though death was always around the corner, and I would stumble into his hooded presence at any time.

On one devilishly cold night I did get a glimpse of death. I was sitting on the floor by the fireplace in my grandparents' home, intently reading a comic book while trying to stay warm. Next to me in chairs sat my mother and grandmother, chatting away about my father, who had just been accepted into medical school in Augusta. It was an exciting time for all of us because it meant that my father would begin that long journey through medical education that would lead to him becoming a doctor.

The two women were so deeply engaged in conversation that they hardly noticed my grandfather as he opened the front door and shivered his way to a spot close to the fireplace. He was wearing his turtle green wool coat and a cap, but it didn't seem to be doing the job of keeping him warm. He just stood there and shivered, standing as close to the fire as he could.

"What's wrong, hon?" asked my grandmother.

"I don't know," said my grandfather. "I've never felt colder in my life than tonight."

The two women continued to talk, and my grandfather continued to shiver. Finally, at my grandmother's suggestion, he went to bed, where he could bury himself beneath piles of blankets.

When I awoke the next day I could hear my mother and grandmother talking very loud downstairs and crying. I peeked out of my room and could see both of them going in and out of my grandparents' room. Shortly thereafter, the front door opened, and my father came in, leading two ambulance attendants with a stretcher.

My father embraced my mother for comfort and looked at me as I started to come out of my room.

"Stay there a minute, Raymond," he said to me. I stayed at the top of the stairs until my grandfather was wheeled out of the house, and then I ran down.

"I think your grandfather has had a stroke," said my grandmother.

Stroke. The word meant nothing to me, but I began to cry. Soon
we were all weeping and holding one another. Then my father
said that he and Grandmother would follow the ambulance to the
hospital and Mother and I should stay home.

Stroke, I repeated to myself. *Stroke.* I had no idea what it was,
but I was certain that I was never going to see my grandfather
again. I went into a kind of shock that erased my memory of the
next few days. Even now I can't remember if I went to the hospital to see him; nor can I remember the day he returned from the
hospital. Strangely enough, I do remember reliving my short life
with the man who was most important to me.

For instance, I remember looking at a blue marble on my
bedroom dresser and being able to recall the day my grandfather
gave it to me. I had been with my aunt May, who picked us up every Saturday in a cab and took me downtown to buy me a toy. On
this particular day we got out of the cab right next to a pipe that
was standing up about two inches from the edge of the sidewalk.
While my aunt paid the cab, I looked down into the pipe and saw a
blue cat's-eye marble sitting at the bottom. I tried and tried to get
that marble, but my short fingers couldn't quite reach it.

When my aunt took my hand and walked me into the toy store,
I thought I would never see that marble again. But when we came
out of the store, there was my grandfather with the marble in his
hand and a smile on his face. Now with him in the hospital with a
stroke, all I could think of was his face beaming down at me as he
held the marble that was as bright and friendly as his jovial blue
eyes and wonderful smile.

Stroke. Was my grandfather being punished for having me call
him Daddy when my father was away at war? Was he being pun-

ished for being so totally devoted to me? At times I wondered if the stroke was my fault for thinking of my grandfather as my dad.

Stroke. Or maybe it was my father's fault? Maybe the way my father treated me—a great source of distress for my grandfather—had caused the stroke. Did their bad relationship somehow cause this calamity? I know it made me feel confused, guilty, and sick to my stomach. Was a stroke the same kind of sickness? I was totally confused.

My grandfather's stroke was so distressing to me that I can't remember how long it was before he returned. Thinking back, I do remember coming down the stairs one morning and having my grandmother take my hand and lead me into their bedroom. There, propped up with pillows, was Granddad. He couldn't speak, although he tried, and when he smiled only half of his mouth curled up; the other half remained immobile. His left hand didn't work, and neither did his left leg. Rather, those two limbs just lay there like they were dead.

When I realized that half of my grandfather didn't work, I began to fidget nervously and cry. It was horrifying to see the man I thought so highly of in such a condition. A dozen questions popped into my mind. Was my grandfather still in there, just trapped inside a nonfunctioning body? Was this just temporary? Would he ever be okay again? And what is a stroke anyway?

As these questions ran through my mind I began to cry very hard. Then I noticed that my grandfather's working eye was becoming damp with tears that ran down his cheek. I wanted to touch him, but I was afraid that I might hurt him. Mercifully, my grandmother intervened.

"Come on, Raymond," she said, putting her arm around me and walking me out of the room. "Grandpa needs a lot of rest."

The experience of seeing my grandfather was so traumatizing that I remember very little of my grandfather after the stroke. Most of the time he stayed in bed, looking at the ceiling, at the wall, or out the window, depending upon which way he was turned in bed. Sometimes Uncle Fairley would come over, and he and my grandmother would lift Grandfather into an old-fashioned wheelchair and take him out to the porch, where he sat slumped and silent. It seemed as though those were the only places I saw my grandfather for the next eight years. And since he was paralyzed, my interactions with him were very limited.

My grief is apparent to me now, looking back. I had lost my best friend, a man who had insulated me from what was bad about the world and introduced me to what was good. Now that he was essentially gone, there was little for me to do. My father spent all of his time studying for his medical school tests, my mother focused her attentions on his needs, Grandmother was taking care of Grandfather, and no one talked about how they felt about the loss of the family patriarch.

Nowadays the phrase "family dysfunction" would come up in discussing this situation, but in 1948 the concept was not yet defined and the phrase was not yet in the medical lexicon. In retrospect, I see that our family was truly dysfunctional, but oddly normal for the times.

With the loss of my grandfather, my curiosity veered in other directions. I spent a lot of time with the few other children in town my age, but soon became bored with children's games. I was more curious than these other children and had little interest in activities that didn't have creative elements to them.

I remember standing at the mouth of the caves on the outskirts of Porterdale and having an uncanny feeling, like I was about to step into the mouth of the world. Even at such an early age, I felt that these earth openings provided access to something deep inside of us. When I expressed this feeling to the other children, they gave me a blank look, clearly not understanding what I was talking about.

My playmates complained to their parents that I was boring, and to them I definitely was. But as our neighbor Mrs. Crowell said to her son Billy, "Raymond Jr. is going to be somebody very special. He's the smart kid, and maybe you should learn from him."

With my mind in creative turmoil, I began to turn inward. I saw words as the key to the intellectual world and began to work on my reading ability. At breakfast I would look at the backs of cereal boxes and ask whoever was at the table with me how to pronounce words and what they meant. Before long, I was reading cereal boxes with little effort and decided to advance to more difficult reading material, namely, comic books. I had looked at Donald Duck comics in the past, but now I was making an effort to actually read them. And I did. Before the end of my fourth birthday I was reading several Donald Duck comics per week, fully engrossed in the genius of the creator, Carl Barks.

In many ways, Barks replaced my grandfather. I can honestly say that he became one of the biggest figures in my life. I knew the exact day each month when the next Donald Duck comic would come out. To this day I can remember the excitement of buying them and the fresh smell of the ink as I opened them and began to read the stories.

I know it seems odd to hear an adult admit that comic book figures helped shape his life. But in recent years I have read that both Steven Spielberg and George Lucas, two of my generation's greatest film directors, had their sense of adventure shaped by the works of Carl Barks. I am sure they can point to specific comic books that were seminal in their lives. I know I certainly can.

It was to Carl Barks and my father that I owe my eventual career path. I was reading a comic book in the same room where my father sat reading his anatomy book. Suddenly I came across the word "philosopher." I believe Donald was pretending to be a philosopher, and for the life of me I didn't know what that word meant. I am sure I mutilated the word the first time I said it, but I looked up at my dad and asked, "What is a philosopher?"

My dad didn't look up from his book, but his answer was clear and to the point.

"Philosophers are very wise men who talk about very big and important questions," he said.

"Then that's what I want to be," I said. At the age of four, I knew clearly that I wanted to answer the world's big questions, no matter what those questions might be. I wanted to become a philosopher.

Having begun this chapter with my grandfather's stroke, I will end it with his death. Although he didn't die for another eight years, he was essentially gone from my life after that stroke. He couldn't chase me in the yard anymore or take long walks with me and talk about the people he knew or the places he had been. And although he tried to read to me a few times, he gave up on that too, since he couldn't form the words that he was looking at on the pages of books that I turned for him.

Grandmother, trying to make the best of the situation, would say that he was only half-broken, since the stroke had affected half of his body. But even at the age of four I could see that Grandpa was less than half there. The change in him was so fast and so definite that I often likened it to turning off a light switch.

Turn it on and the room goes bright, turn it off and the room is dark. His light had been turned off and nothing—not Grandma, not modern medicine, not prayer, and not my dad—could turn it on again. My grandfather had become a dark room.

For the next eight years, my grandmother was totally devoted to her husband. She bathed him, helped him with the bedpan, turned him over frequently to prevent bed sores, and sat with him on the porch. When Fairley or my father helped her get him seated in the antique wheelchair, she would wheel him through the house, out the front door, and down the street for a "roll."

Conversation after the stroke became one-sided between them. Grandmother would read him newspapers or magazines or talk about events in Porterdale, and he would sit silent and listen. Sometimes he would just fall asleep and she would keep talking as though he were as attentive as ever. When he smiled, half of his face worked. When he tried to speak, half of his tongue worked, as did—it seemed—half of his mental functions. It was the ultimate horror for all of us.

When Grandfather died in 1956, my grandmother seemed to expect it. She called the Porterdale Funeral Home and the owner, Mr. Davis, drove the home's vehicle over himself, loaded my grandfather's body on a stretcher, and returned to the home to prepare the body for burial.

We returned for the funeral from Macon, where we were living. When we went to the funeral home, Mr. Davis took my mother's arm in his and with tears in his eyes told her that her father had no bed sores on his body—"not one"—until the day he died.

"We were astounded," he said, looking deeply into my mother's eyes. "Can you imagine? He couldn't turn over or take care of himself in any way for eight years, and still he had no bed sores. Your mother's a saint."

CHAPTER THREE

I wouldn't say that I focused excessively on death as a child, but when the subject came up I could rarely keep my questions to myself. For example, there was the first time I truly pondered the notion that death may be survivable.

It was the summer of 1956 in Macon, Georgia, and I was twelve years old. I was standing at the corner of our house by the garage waiting for my father to come home. It wasn't unusual for him to be late. He was a surgeon, and even at my young age I knew that there was no nine-to-five in that profession. Nevertheless, I was waiting anxiously by the garage for him because we were planning a weekend in the woods at a cabin my mother had rented.

Finally I could see his big Oldsmobile come around the corner and lumber down the street. He pulled the car onto the carport and steered the front end within a foot or so of my legs. It always made me nervous when he did this, but I didn't move, even though getting tapped by the massive car's bumper would be painful. I held my ground.

Dad got out of the car and took a deep breath, like it was the first he'd had all day. Then he smiled, which made me think he was feeling guilty for being late, and shut his car door. I noticed that he was wearing no tie or jacket, and his longish crew cut looked slightly mussed, as though he had been running his hands through it.

"Sorry I'm late," he said. "But right before I was about to leave a patient's heart stopped and I had to start it again."

My father was a natural surgeon who loved what he did and talked about it at every opportunity. Typical dinner conversations included how to stop a spurting aneurysm or the many different and fascinating ways to set a badly broken leg. That evening, he began to explain the process of restarting a heart, which was vastly different in those days before chest compression became the norm or the defibrillator was invented.

"By the time I got to the man he was dead," said my father, who described the next step of cutting open the man's chest by drawing his finger across the chest of an imaginary patient in front of him. "I cut open his chest just below his breastbone and was able to get my hand in there and squeeze his heart until it started beating again."

The discussion of such an act could easily have been traumatizing to a twelve-year-old, but I was used to hearing the physical details of medical emergencies. That day, however, my father's words hit me in a slightly different way. My mind stuck on one thing my father said: "The man was dead."

At that age, the idea of an afterlife would not have occurred to me. I had made up my mind even earlier in my life that when you die your body goes to nothing and your consciousness simply vanishes.

But now, as Dad told me about reviving this man's heart that had stopped beating, I remember saying, "Do you mean that he was dead?"

My father seemed taken aback by the way I had formulated the situation. I seriously doubt that he had considered what it was like for the patient, who had been resurrected from certain death by my father's deft handiwork. I could see my father thinking for a moment about my question, and then he shook it off. "Yeah, the man was dead, but I brought him back to life."

I didn't hear any more of what my father said. All I could think about was what this experience must have been like for the patient. I remember thinking that this man must have been in the darkest, deepest, most unfathomable and utter blackness—and then he had come back from that. Did he know he was dead when he was dead? Would he be able to tell us what that other place was like? Or was there another place at all? This man had been in a place of total obliteration, yet he returned. *Was there anything we could learn from that?*

"Dad, did you talk to the patient when he came back?" I asked. "Where did he go when he died?"

"Well, I did talk to him," my father said, somewhat defensively. "But not about that. I asked him if he knew his name and if he could count the number of fingers I was holding up. That seemed more important at the time."

I was only twelve years old at the time, so I was puzzled as to why my questions about the look and location of the afterlife disturbed my father so much. It didn't become clear until much later, when I was a student in one of Professor Marshall's philosophy classes at the University of Virginia, just exactly why my father didn't consider the discussion of the afterlife to be a "live op-tion." William James, the nineteenth-century psychologist and philosopher who coined this phrase in *Varieties of Religious Experience*, his great book on the origin and purpose of religion from the psychological point of view, defined a live option as religious belief that we can relate to, usually because it has been with us from childhood. So, for example, Hinduism was not a live option for James because it was not a part of his childhood experience and he had no familiarity with it. Christianity, on the other hand, was a live option for James because he had been exposed to Christian ideas as a young person.

My father had been raised an atheist and was dubious about religion, to say the least. The notion of an afterlife was not a live option for him. In fact, he would become agitated at the mere discussion of religion, calling it institutionalized superstition, or worse. Just mentioning something like the afterlife to him, if he was in the wrong mood, could dampen the discussion with a truckload of invective. So concerned was I about his ridicule that it took me years to realize that notions of the afterlife can exist independent of religion. In fact, I can now say with assurance that "religion" and "afterlife" are two entirely different concepts linked together only by religious dogma.

To be fair to my father, survival of bodily death didn't seem like a live option to me at the time either. It never entered my mind that this man who died had stepped into some kind of an afterlife dimension. What I was fascinated by was that he had been in a state of total obliteration and then come back. The idea that something had been going on while he was dead, that perhaps he was out of his body watching my father perform this desperate procedure to save his life, did not cross my mind. Now I realize that he may have been having the peak experience of his lifetime.

He may even have confided later to his wife that he left the room via a tunnel of light and met dead relatives who convinced him that a spiritual life awaited his passage from the physical realm.

Years later, when I began to hear about near-death experiences for the first time, I thought of the man my father had saved by plunging his experienced hands into his patient's chest. I remember thinking, *Would my father have heard a story like this if he had thought to ask the patient whose heart he had revived?*

About this time my parents enrolled me in Stratford Academy, a private school started for gifted children. The school was in an antebellum mansion overlooking Macon from the top of a hill. The facility was beautiful, with a Victorian house as the main building and a large brick carriage house that held classrooms and a library.

The headmaster was Joe Hill, who became one of the most influential people in my life. He was a historian who demanded much from his students. On the first day of school he came to class with a stack of thirteen books and assigned one to each of us in the class. I was lucky enough to be assigned Thucydides' work on the Peloponnesian War. I was in the eleventh grade.

Mrs. Hill was just as amazing as her husband. We studied literature under her, and every week the thirteen members of the class had to write a lengthy paper about what they had read. With the close personal attention we received from the Hills and other staff members at Stratford Academy, none of this work was difficult, even though we were so young.

All of a sudden I was getting straight As on my report card. I was no longer derogatorily labeled "the smart kid," as I had been by the other students at the public high school. Now, at Stratford, I was among the smart kids in an environment that truly respected intellect. I had finally found the place where I belonged, and I was thriving. My depression left me, and my parents noted that I rarely retreated to the basement for long periods of time anymore, something I had done frequently when I was in public school.

My parents made a lot of my "return to normal," and I can now understand why. After all, how many sixteen-year-olds are interested in constant, self-guided study? Not many. Was it abnormal? Perhaps so to an outside observer, but from my point of view I was not abnormal. I liked to learn the way most boys like to play baseball.

There was something going on that was definitely abnormal, however, and that was my body temperature. Despite the heat of the Georgia summers and the hot furnaces and thick coats of the winters, I always felt constantly and memorably chilled to the bone and had a "funny feeling" in my throat, a tingling that was difficult to describe. I also had other feelings that are easier to sum up. I felt as though everything around me was a dream, and that I was watching someone else's reality. It was like there was glass between me and the rest of the world and a feeling of derealization. This was an annoying feeling, one that I always knew was wrong but that I could not shake.

I think these feelings were the first signs of the thyroid deficiency—myxedema—that plagues me to this day. Most people have never heard of this disease. Myxedema is caused by an underactive thyroid gland, one that does not produce enough thyroxine. This hormone controls much of a person's metabolism. If one has too much thyroxine—hyperthyroidism—then the body's metabolism burns at a high rate. People with hyperthyroidism have unpleasant symptoms such as weight loss, fast heart rate, increased bowel movements, heat intolerance, and insomnia.

On the other end of the spectrum, people with too little thyroxine—hypothyroidism, which is what I have—are plagued by low metabolism, cold intolerance, fatigue, hair loss, depression, and irritability. If hypothyroidism continues, then myxedema madness can occur, a condition that leads progressively to dementia and delirium and eventually to hallucinations or psychosis.

At this point in my young life, I was far from suffering myxedema madness, but I was certainly at the beginning stages of hypothyroidism. The problem was that nobody knew it. To most people I just came across as an aloof and physically heavy young man who was mainly concerned with books and much less concerned with the world around him. In reality, though, I was a person with a developing thyroid problem that left me with little physical energy and a diminished ability to push back against the world.

Oddly enough, my thyroid problem may have been diagnosed at this time by my uncle Carter. I remember the moment well. My father and I were with Carter, standing outside a Walgreen's drugstore in downtown Macon, when Carter put his hand on my arm and then put the back of his hand against my face. A frown came over his face as he tapped my father on the arm.

"I think Ray has thyroid problems," he said. "He should be sweating like the rest of us, but he's as cool as a cucumber."

My dad reached over and put his hand on my face. I noticed that he was perspiring just as heavily as one would expect on a hot and humid summer afternoon in the Deep South. Uncle Carter was pouring sweat too, his shirt soaked like he had walked past a sprinkler.

As my father's hand touched my face, the front door of the Walgreen's drugstore opened and the cool air from the air-conditioned store blew out the door and across my dry and cold body.

"I think it's just the air conditioning from the store," he said.

The two doctors engaged in a brief conversation about my case. My uncle asked me if I ever had a "funny feeling" in my throat. When I said yes, he started feeling my throat and asked if I had gained weight or ever felt cold when I thought I should be hot.

As I started answering his questions he became more interested. Then the Walgreen's door swung open and out came my mother and aunt.

"Come on, let's go," said my aunt. "It's hot out here."

Now, when I think of the attitude I adopted in those days toward knowledge, I think of the philosopher Kant, who said, "There are always two things that fill me with wonder—the starry heavens above me and the conscious self within me." That is how it was for me as I found myself engrossed in the worlds of astronomy and human psychology.

My interest in the starry heavens came one day in 1952 when I was perusing the racks at a newsstand in a downtown hotel. I frequently became lost in the world of magazine covers and current news, but on this day a headline on the cover of *Collier's* magazine caught my eye: "Man Will Fly in Space Soon." That article, which would change my life, was written by a man with the unpronounceable name of Werner von Braun. Working for Hitler during World War II, he had developed the V-2 rocket, which at the time was an advanced weapon that was launched from sites in Europe at his great nemesis, Great Britain. These deadly winged "buzz bombs," as the British called them, would fall from the sky with their explosive payload. They killed very few people, but their presence was unnerving to the British, who hated not only the bombs but the men like von Braun who had created them.

When the war ended, the United States scooped von Braun and other scientists out of Germany and brought them here to start our own rocket program. Von Braun was our greatest scientific catch from the war. A genius and a natural leader, von Braun was in charge of the American rocket program that eventually put a man on the moon and sent spacecrafts far beyond it. One NASA source called von Braun, "without a doubt, the greatest rocket scientist in history."

The article I found at the newsstand that day presented a brief history of rockets. Over the next several issues the magazine covered such enticing subjects as the satellites that had already been launched, the creation of three-stage rockets that would blast men into outer space, the creation of giant space stations, flights to the moon, and the eventual creation of winged airplanes that would fly into outer space.

I was already hooked on astronomy at this time. But this series of magazine articles made me realize that we were close to being able to leave the earth and study firsthand many of the things we had only seen with telescopes or speculated about. As I read these articles I was in complete ecstasy.

After the second part of this space travel series came out, I showed my father what I was reading. I remember the event very well, because it was the beginning of another rift between us. He was sitting in his easy chair, reading the newspapers, when I proudly opened the magazines and showed him the articles. I expected to have a conversation with him about the eventual exploration of outer space, so I was surprised to hear him chuckle as he scanned the magazine pages.

"This is completely ridiculous," he said, tossing the magazines at my feet. "Man will never go to the moon!"

For the next fifteen years my father tormented me with his belief that man would never go to the moon. He made fun of my belief until the day Neil Armstrong took his first step on the moon, and then he never mentioned it again.

Looking back, I think that my father either thought I was mentally ill to believe "such nonsense" or perhaps believed that I would waste my life studying the heavens when there was so much here on earth that deserved our focus. Beyond making it clear that he was completely against any interest I had in space travel, he never really told me what his issue was with it.

Afraid that my father would throw out the magazines, I kept them hidden under my mattress, like many boys who hide *Playboy*. Late at night I would bring them out and read them by flashlight, using them to prime myself for dreams of weightlessness or a deep space view of our own world.

I kept the magazines for years. Finally they deteriorated so much from constant reading that I had to tape their covers to keep them together. I eventually lost them when I went to college.

I couldn't get enough of astronomy. The vastness of space and the fact that there might be other worlds out there, the pictures of Mars with the lacework of canals covering its red surface, the pictures of Saturn and the notion that in my lifetime we could fly to these distant planets—all of these things became my primary source of daydreams. I would sit at my desk during school and imagine flying in space. By the end of the day my notebook would be filled with different designs for spacecraft. I would imagine sitting in the pilot's seat, feeling the g-forces as the rocket blasted off. Then I would be weightless as the spacecraft shot across the universe. Sometimes I would take a short trip to the moon. But if time allowed, I would imagine going all the way to Mars, where a soft landing would allow me to see up close the canals that I had only seen in photographs. Sometimes, in my mind, living beings came out of those canals to greet me and I would be treated to a visit with people from another planet.

When this outer space obsession began, I was afraid that the teacher might call on me and I would be brought back into the gravity of the classroom. After a while, though, I didn't care if the teacher called on me, no matter how embarrassed I might be not to know what she had been talking about. I was an astronaut— an astronaut of inner space at this point, but an explorer nonetheless.

Other thoughts came to my mind too. I realized that we were one of perhaps thousands or tens of thousands of planets. Thinking about the vastness of space expanded my consciousness. It became obvious to me that among these uncountable galaxies, we could not be the only living beings. Somewhere out in space, there were more of us. I began to draw the types of people we might encounter on other planets. The ones on larger planets might have a squat appearance from the increased pull of gravity, while those on smaller planets would be spindly and tall because they would not need very much muscle. These basic illustrations were of great interest to my teachers, who always paused to look as they walked past my desk.

I was also drawn to science fiction movies, all of which had aliens who disembarked from spaceships and either wreaked havoc on earth or came in peace.

For some reason, my father would become very upset when I chose to go to a science fiction film. When I asked him for my allowance to go to a movie, I could see his face start to flush red and his teeth clench.

"You're wasting your money on that garbage," he said. "There's more to do here that you should focus on. Outer space is just an excuse to daydream. You should think about things that are here on earth!"

The psyches of other kids might have been damaged by this kind of treatment from their father. It had little effect on me, however. That my father couldn't see the great future in space exploration just made me feel sorry for him. I equate his attitude with that of many parents nowadays who can't see the infinite possibilities for their children in playing video games and cruising the Internet. Sometimes the future is in daydreaming or play.

By now I had developed male role models. At this point in my life most of them were scientists, and the man at the top of the list was Werner von Braun. So I was beside myself in March 1958 when I picked up the Macon newspaper and read the headline, "Famed Dr. von Braun to Speak in Macon."

On the night of his lecture I dressed in my nicest clothing and went to the college auditorium to hear my idol. The spacecraft *Explorer 1*, the first earth satellite to be launched by the United States, had just been sent into space a month earlier, so I expected a big crowd. But when I arrived, the auditorium was only about half full. I sat up front as von Braun talked about the space program, his enthusiasm and accent making him difficult to comprehend.

I approached von Braun when the lecture was over and engaged him in a conversation about the difficulties of space travel. We spoke for maybe half an hour, and then one of his handlers broke in and told him his car was waiting. Von Braun reached out and shook my hand. "What is your name again?" he asked, repeating it when I told him.

Six years later he returned to Macon, this time to Mercer College, where the auditorium was filled to capacity. The Mercury space program was in full swing at that point, and there were few things more interesting to Americans than rockets, astronauts, and von Braun.

After his talk, I approached the podium to thank him for an excellent presentation. There were dozens of students around him, but when he saw me approaching he waded through them and stuck out his big hand.

"Raymond Moody," he said. "How are you?"

I beamed for weeks when that happened. I had made an impression on a great genius. I must have been on the right track.

CHAPTER FOUR

⌒

B y the time I left high school, my focus in life had become the unfathomable universe. My passion since age
seven had been astronomy. The formation of the universe
through (possibly) a "big bang" and the notion that the clockwork
of planets and stars and asteroids, comets, black holes, and whatever else was governed by powerful and invisible physical laws
provided enough for my mind to ponder for the rest of my life.
As the late Carl Sagan said, "What makes the universe so hard to
comprehend is that there's nothing to compare it with."

I genuinely felt that way about astronomy when I graduated
from high school, and I searched hard for the best school for
astronomy before finally settling on the University of Virginia.
Founded by Thomas Jefferson, who felt that the South needed a
first-class school, UVA represents a living memorial to the great
intellect of our third president. Jefferson's home, Monticello, is

located about five miles from the campus, and the ghost of this great president has been seen there many times.

Jefferson founded the university in 1819 in part because he wanted to establish an institution for the study of astronomy, which he considered to be as important a discipline as architecture. Coming from Jefferson, this is saying something, given that he designed several buildings, including Monticello, which is surely one of the most beautiful personal residences in the United States.

Astronomy was practiced almost as a hobby at the university while Jefferson and then his successors struggled to find and fund the right professors. It wasn't until 1870, forty-four years after Jefferson's death, that Leander McCormick arrived at UVA to launch a truly first-rate "school of the heavens." The astronomy program has been a jewel in UVA's crown ever since.

I enrolled in the UVA Department of Astronomy in the hope of becoming an astronomer. But within weeks it became clear to me that I would not be spending my time at the eyepiece of a telescope. Instead, I discovered philosophy and logic, which introduced me to a level of thought I had not known existed.

The first class to do this was a liberal arts seminar. I was in the scholars' program, so I was allowed to be in this elite program that involved reading the classics and dissecting them in class with the professors. Our first semester was a veritable festival of reading: we read *The Iliad*, *The Odyssey*, several plays by Sophocles, Aeschylus, Euripides, and Aristophanes, Plato's *Ion*, *Apology of Socrates*, *Crito*, and *Phaedo*, the *Histories* of Herodotus, Thucydides's *History of the Peloponnesian War*, and Aristotle's *Poetics*.

If that course allowed me to set sail on a sea of thought, a philosophy class pulled me into truly deep water. Our goal in this class was to read two books: Plato's *Republic* and *The Affluent So-*

ciety by John Kenneth Galbraith. I found Galbraith's book to be a fascinating exploration of affluence in post–World War II America, but it was Plato's *Republic* that swept me away. I remember where I was when that life-changing event took place, and even the time of day. It was 12:30 at the UVA library. Sitting alone at a big wooden table, I broke out *The Republic* and began reading.

In the first few pages, Socrates is talking to Cephalus, an older businessman who has finished his career and is now searching for spiritual enlightenment. Now, at the end of his life, Cephalus can see death coming, and thoughts and questions about the afterlife are filling his head. To paraphrase the dialogue between Cephalus and Socrates:

"I've done well in my life," he tells Socrates. "But now I am closer to dying and my mind goes back to all of the things I've heard about the afterlife [or the "underworld," which is where the Greeks assumed the afterlife takes place] and I am agonizing about this. Is there an afterlife?"

Socrates thinks a moment and then steers the conversation in another direction. He lauds Cephalus for his long life and then asks him what he thinks is the meaning of justice. Cephalus considers this question and then says, with confidence, "Justice is returning to someone what you owe to them." I remember reading that and thinking that such a definition seemed plausible.

Socrates thinks so too, for a few minutes at least. He once again speaks in laudatory terms about the wisdom displayed by Cephalus, only this time he adds a twist.

"What if a friend of yours comes to you and gives you a knife," says Socrates. "And that friend asks you to keep this knife for him and to return it when he comes back from his voyage to another town. When he returns, the friend is not the same person. His hair is mussed up, his eyes are blazing, and he is babbling, talking out of his head and making no sense. Very clearly, he asks you to return his knife. Cephalus, my friend, would it be justice to return that knife to him? Under those circumstances, do you owe that knife to him?"

For a moment I closed the book. I looked up at the sunlight streaming into the library from one of the side windows and felt its warmth—and yes, its enlightenment. It may sound vain, but the first thing that appealed to me in Plato's *Republic* was the way Socrates could take apart anybody's argument. What became obvious to me immediately was that Socrates dealt not only with truth and untruth but also with that vast gray area in between. I began a simple list of questions that occupied that gray area between right and wrong, between truth and lies: *Is it justice to return the knife to this man? . . . Is war ever justified? . . . Is it ever okay to let a patient take his own life?* The longer that list got, the clearer it became to me that I needed to know and follow the reasoning of Socrates in order to take the rigidity out my own thought processes.

I felt it was important to be able to think like Socrates. After all, when people start philosophizing, they often work themselves into a corner from which they cannot escape. For instance, if you hold to a definition of justice as returning to someone what you owe him or her, you will quickly encounter questions like the one posed to Cephalus.

A philosopher's job is to provide course correction to an argument that doesn't make sense—not out of spite or a sense of superiority, but in the spirit of helpfulness. Of course, as Socrates realized, not everyone is amenable to a philosopher's help. Some people get hostile or no longer view the philosopher as a friend. After all, once that person points out that nonsense is just a few reasoning steps away from a "solid" argument, he or she is likely to offend those who are dogmatic or thin-skinned. But losing such friends is the risk of being a philosopher.

There was another thing that drew me to Socrates, and that was the fearless way in which he wrestled with mankind's most important question: *What happens when we die?*

At this point in my young life, my interest in the question of an afterlife was like my interest in studying black holes in astronomy: though many astronomers believed that black holes exist somewhere out there in the vast universe, they had been unable to prove that black holes exist or describe how they work. I felt that the question of the afterlife was the black hole of the personal universe: something for which substantial proof of existence had been offered but which had not yet been explored in the proper way by scientists and philosophers.

Socrates was doing that very thing in *The Republic*. Everybody knows that *The Republic* is about justice. But at its heart it is really about justice *and* what justice is in relation to life after death. At the very beginning, Cephalus brings up the notion of life after death, which frames the entire work in the notion that justice is related to the afterlife.

But it was the story told about the soldier Ur by Socrates at the end of Plato's *Republic* that truly kindled my interest in answering questions about the afterlife. Ur was a warrior who was believed to be dead on the battlefield. Soldiers cleaning up the battlefield threw him on a stack of his dead comrades for disposal. Several days later, as friends were preparing the funeral pyre, Ur suddenly sat up and announced that he had been to the other world.

"He said that when his soul left the body he went on a journey with a great company," says Socrates,

and that they came to a mysterious place at which there were two openings in the earth; they were near together, and over against them were two other openings in the heaven above. In the intermediate space there were judges seated. . . . He drew near, and they told him that he was to be the messenger who would carry the report of the other-world to men, and they bade him hear and see all that was to be heard and seen in that place. Then he beheld and saw on one side the souls departing at either opening of heaven and earth when sentence had been given on them; and at the two other openings other souls, some ascending out of the earth dusty and worn with travel, some descending out of heaven clean and bright. And arriving ever and anon they seemed to have come from a long journey, and they went forth with gladness into the meadow, where they encamped as at a festival; and those who knew one another embraced and conversed, the souls which came from earth curiously enquiring about the things above, and the souls which came from heaven about the things beneath. And they told one another of what had happened by the way, those from below weeping and sorrowing at the remembrance of the things which they had endured and seen in their journey beneath the earth . . . while those from above were describing heavenly delights and visions of inconceivable beauty.

By the time I finished Plato's *Republic*, I was truly hooked on philosophy. I left the library that day realizing that destiny had turned me into an astronaut of inner space, one who would now explore the inner universe of thought instead of the universe outside of our earth.

My readings for the liberal arts seminar carried on into the second semester, when we read the classics of science: Paracelsus's *The Treasure of Treasures for the Alchemist*, Boyle's *The Skeptical Chemist*, Lavoisier's *Elements of Chemistry*, the periodic table of the elements, Lucretius's *On Nature*, Galileo's dialogues about his experiments, Newton's *Philosophiae Naturalis Principia Mathematica*, Einstein's treatment of the theory of relativity, Euclid's *Elements*, Bernard's *Experimental Medicine*, Mendel's original paper on heredity, and Darwin's *Descent of Man*.

I was constantly reading. And as my classmates and I read all of this work and discussed it in Dr. Marcus Mallett's excellent class, the information about the universe that I had spent years absorbing was now coming back into my own consciousness through philosophy. I remember realizing that I was little more than a spot of consciousness in an immense universe of nonsense. As French dramatist Georges Battaille said, "Nonsense is the end result of all sense."

During this period, thoughts of studying the afterlife were always in my head. In *Clouds*, Aristophanes mentions that Socrates was adept at calling up the dead. In *The Odyssey*, there is the very powerful scene where Odysseus visits the underworld. All of this came together with a reading of Herodotus, who writes about the Oracle of the Dead in Acheron, which is where Socrates was calling up the dead, according to Aristophanes. For the Greeks, the direction of the afterlife was down, toward somewhere in the underworld. It was plausible, they believed, to go down into a labyrinth of caves known as Oracles of the Dead and see one's dead relatives. The Greeks felt that there were a number of ways in which the underworld could be visited. One was happenstance: A man could be walking through the woods when suddenly the ground beneath his feet would crumble and he would find himself deep in a cave. If he made it back alive, he could tell of what he had seen in the afterlife. Another way to enter the next life was to visit one of these caves or Oracles, where a priest would take the initiate on a sort of tour of the afterlife. Another way was to be like the soldier Ur—to die and return. Of these three methods—happenstance, the guided tour, and the near-death of Ur—the one Socrates truly believed was the story of Ur, which he described as "but the tale of a warrior bold."

All three of these methods of visiting the afterlife are dealt with in *The Republic*. I began to wonder with great excitement: *Did the ancient Greeks have a way of venturing into the afterlife and connecting with departed loved ones? Did they have actual techniques to make these connections?* I filed these questions away for further consideration.

What happens when we die?

That was clearly the most important question for Socrates, and therefore it became the most important question for me. Even as a freshman in college, I was certain that I was embarking on some kind of quest to find the answer.

CHAPTER FIVE

⌒

At the end of my second year as a philosophy student, I was called into Professor David Yalden-Thompson's office. Ever since the first time I was called to the principal's office, it has made me nervous to be summoned by a person in a superior position. But on this day I had little to be concerned about. Professor Yalden-Thompson was all smiles as he offered a chair for me to sit in and then sat down himself in his creaky wooden office chair. He got right to the point.

"Raymond, we want you to join the honors program in philosophy."

I didn't know what to say. Of course I had heard of the honors program, but like receiving a Nobel Prize or winning the lottery, it was something that happened to other people.

Being asked to join the honors program was an amazing experience, especially to someone like me who had spent so much of his childhood down in the basement reading. What it meant was that I would spend the last two years of my college career with only one duty: I would do nothing but read.

Professor Yalden-Thompson gave me the particulars. For three of those four semesters I would be with a different philosophy professor. I would meet with the professor once a week for a tutorial to discuss one of three philosophical disciplines: epistemology (the study of the nature of knowledge), metaphysics (the study of the nature of being and beings), and ethics (the study of moral standards). Finally, I would have an entire semester in which to write my honors thesis.

To someone whose two favorite activities are reading and thinking, this sounded like a dream assignment. And it was. But it wasn't easy.

All of the reading assignments were accompanied by writing assignments. On a weekly basis, honors students had to write a long paper on what sometimes seemed to be an unfathomable philosophical concept. When we finished the paper, we had to sit with our professor for that semester and *read* the paper out loud to him. It was excruciating. Every few words the professor would stop the reading and ask for specifics about what we had written: *What do you mean by "improbable but likely"? Did you really mean to use the word "absolute"?*

I would go into these one-on-one sessions with a deep feeling of fear in my stomach. Within a few of these sessions, however, I began to go in with a feeling of excitement as I realized that the professors were there to help me and that their questions weren't antagonistic but rather were aimed at challenging me and keeping me on an intellectual path. And although I jokingly referred to them as "intellectual thrashings," I didn't truly believe that was what these one-on-one sessions were about. I came to feel that these meetings with my professors gave me the best education I could have.

On top of all this, there was another benefit to being in the honors program: We could audit any class on campus at any time. We could walk into an ancient history class, an evolutionary biology class, or an American government class, introduce ourselves to the professor, and be allowed to sit down and listen to what he had to say. We didn't have to read for the course or take tests. In an honors class you are considered a self-learner, and that is how all the professors on campus treated us.

I began auditing graduate philosophy courses. One of those courses was the philosophical topics course taught by Professors John Marshall and Peter Heath. The topic in one of these evening classes was the question of the afterlife. To explore this question the class had read two works: Plato's *Phaedo*, possibly the best book ever written on the afterlife from a rational point of view, and David Hume's essay on immortality.

On one of the nights I was in the class, Dr. Marshall read Hume's thesis statement, noting that this powerful commentary on the provability of the afterlife could be used to argue either side of the life-after-death argument:

> By the mere light of reason it seems impossible to prove the immortality of the soul. Some new species of logic is required for that purpose and some new faculties of the mind that they may enable us to comprehend that logic.

When Dr. Marshall asked what we thought of this, I raised my hand. Given that Hume was an ironist, he obviously thought that proving life after death was not possible. There was even a chance that he considered this new "species of logic" to be delusion, I said to the class. And I felt that Hume was right in light of the type of logic that we have. Nevertheless, I had always suspected that he was wrong in that he most likely believed that we could not come up with a new form of logic, that it was equally unlikely that we would come up with some new faculty of the mind, and that after all, Aristotle had done pretty well for 2,300 years.

"However," I said boldly, "both of these are imminently doable. It's just that people get this mental block and they think it can't be done."

There was silence in the class when I finished, and I expected some kind of counterargument from Dr. Marshall. That didn't happen. Instead, he took a moment to ponder what I had said and then—slowly at first—began to talk about a person who would become a formidable force in my life.

"Right there in the medical school is a man who might just agree with you," he said. "There's a man named Dr. George Ritchie, a psychiatrist, who was *pronounced dead*. He had this experience of seeing this light when he died, and then he left his body and the real adventure began."

Dr. Marshall continued to talk, but I didn't really hear what he had to say. My mind stopped at the mention of Dr. Ritchie's great adventure at what could have been the end of his life. I wanted to meet this man.

At this point I have to say that I was intrigued by Dr. Marshall's mention of "the light" in Dr. Ritchie's experience. I had read William James's *Varieties of Religious Experience*, in which he discusses the role of mystical light in religious experiences. Here is one thing James has to say about the mystical light:

He sees, but cannot define the light which bathes him and by means of which he sees the objects which excite his wonder. If we cannot explain physical light, how can we explain the light which is the truth itself? . . . But do you wish, that I should enclose in poor and barren words sentiments which the heart alone can understand?

Interested in these experiences of light, James began to study, among others, those who had nearly died. It is important to collect and study these experiences, James says, because "they represent the closest thing to a microscope of the mind, that is, they show us in drastically enlarged form the normal processes of things."

One such case study came from a patient who was overdosed by anesthetic. After blacking out from an overly generous administration of chloroform, this woman began to see a strong yet different type of light. Here are her own words describing the event:

After the choking and stifling had passed away, I seemed at first in a state of utter blankness; then came flashes of intense light, alternating with blackness, and with a keen vision of what was going on in the room around me, but no sensation of touch. I thought that I was near death; when, suddenly, my soul became aware of God, who was manifestly dealing with me, handling me, so to speak, in an intense personal present reality. I felt him streaming in like light upon me. . . . I cannot describe the ecstasy I felt. Then, as I gradually awoke from the influence of the anesthetics, the old sense of my relation to the world began to return, the new sense of my relation to God began to fade. I suddenly leapt to my feet on the chair where I was sitting, and shrieked out, "It is too horrible, it is too horrible, it is too horrible," meaning that I could not bear this disillusionment. Then I flung myself on the ground, and at last awoke covered with blood, calling to the two surgeons (who were frightened), "Why did you not kill me? Why would you not let me die?"

These case studies included in James's work were intriguing to me. In the events described there, did people actually pass into a nonphysical world? Does this happen to everyone who dies?

These unstudied experiences were a powerful curiosity to me and made me wonder exactly what is happening as people pass over the threshold of death. With George Ritchie, I hoped I would have the chance to talk to someone who had gone as far as one can go and still return to talk about it.

When I went home for Christmas vacation, I had one of those mysterious coincidences that have cropped up frequently in my life. We were all sitting around at dinner when I happened to mention George Ritchie and his return from death.

I knew none of the particulars, so what I had to say was extremely short and devoid of detail. But when I mentioned his name, a strange and distant look came over my father's face.

"George Ritchie . . . George Ritchie," he said, putting his fork down. "Camp Barkeley, Texas, December 1943. Double lobar pneumonia . . . pronounced dead and then came back."

As it turned out, my father had gone through his corpsman training at Camp Barkeley at the same time as George Ritchie. Needless to say, what happened to Ritchie was big news to the medical staff at this Abilene, Texas, outpost. My father called Ritchie a "legend" and said that he was an honest man who "didn't let religion get in the way of being fun." That was quite an endorsement coming from my father.

I could see what my father meant the first time I met Ritchie. He was the student health psychiatrist at UVA and spent a lot of time with the student population. One day I was walking to The Corner, a sandwich shop off campus, and talking to one of my suite-mates about Dr. Ritchie's story. Suddenly Dr. Ritchie himself came around a corner. My suite-mate knew Ritchie and stopped him for a moment to introduce us.

This was the first time I had seen Ritchie, and I remember thinking that he looked very much like an owl, and a wise one at that. He was on his way to a patient conference and had little time to talk. I got the sense in that brief meeting, though, that Ritchie was kindhearted and interested in the student. He also had that look of someone who had just finished a long session of meditation and didn't have a care in the world.

I liked him immediately.

Within a few days I heard that Ritchie was going to speak to a group of students at one of the fraternity houses. I remember walking up the stairs of the house and sitting in the back of the room. Ritchie was standing in front, talking to a few students in the front row. After a couple of minutes, he checked his watch and stood tall, stretching out to his full six-foot-two height. Then with a kind and slow drawl he told the story that would forever change my life.

He began with the part I already knew from my father—that he was in Army basic training when he developed a case of pneumonia that put him in the infirmary. This was a bad time for Ritchie to end up in a hospital bed. Before joining the Army, he had been accepted to medical school in Richmond, Virginia. Encouraged by the Army to attend, Ritchie was supposed to take the weekly train to the medical college on December 24. But now, the day before leaving, he was in a hospital ward feeling sicker than he had ever felt in his life. He was worried, though, that missing the train to Richmond might mean losing his coveted slot in medical school.

Late that night, after hours of bone-racking coughing, Ritchie took his temperature. It was 107 degrees. He panicked and struggled out of bed to get help. The next thing he knew the medical staff was lowering him back into bed and piling blankets on top of his shivering body.

Within a few hours George Ritchie was pronounced dead. The cause: double lobar pneumonia.

"There was little left for them to do," Ritchie told the assembled students. "I could hear the doctor give the order to prep me for the morgue, which was puzzling because I had the sensation of still being alive. I mean, I could hear the guy.

"I knew I had missed the train, and that bothered me immensely. There was nothing more important in my life at that time than going to medical school. I sat up and looked all around in this dark room for my uniform. I couldn't find it and decided that I didn't have any more time to waste.

"I came out of the room into a long hall and started walking to the end where the stairs were. Coming the other way was a ward man whose job it was to supervise that floor. I walked toward him and then—to my surprise—right through him. I didn't know what to think of that, but I also didn't want to stop to think. I knew I had missed my train to Richmond, and that bothered me more than anything, so I kept going.

"I went to the door that led to the outside, and I stepped right through it. Suddenly and without warning, I was up in the air about five hundred feet, flying at an incredible rate of speed.

"I flew for a while and then saw a city on the other side of a wide river. I decided to land there and did so in front of a white corner diner.

"I stood there for a minute or so until one of the patrons came out of the diner and passed by me. 'What city is this?' I asked, to make certain I was headed toward Richmond. The man didn't answer. I followed behind him. 'Excuse me, sir. Can you please tell me what city this is?' He still didn't answer. In fact, it was clear that he didn't even hear me.

"This was the second time that another human being didn't respond to me at all. I was puzzled.

"I went over by a telephone pole and leaned on the guide wire that holds these poles in place. My hand went through the wire just like it wasn't there.

"At that point I realized that I had left something I needed back at the infirmary in Barkeley: my body. I decided that I had to go back and get it.

"I then discovered something very important about not having your body. When you travel out of body, you are not governed by the same laws of time and space. I just thought about being back at Camp Barkeley, and in no time at all I was back, standing in front of the hospital.

"Now I was lost. I had failed to note which ward I was in when I left, so I had to roam around the wards searching for my body from among the soldiers lying there in the beds. I looked and looked for myself, but I couldn't find me. In fact, I found that, in this state, all of the people looked the same.

"I slowed down and began to look closely at the soldiers one at a time. There were quite a few who looked the way I thought

I looked, but none of them had my black onyx fraternity ring on their finger.

"I became desperate after a while and for a moment thought that somehow my body had been disposed of and I would never find it again. Did that mean I would roam the earth for years, walking through walls and people and never being able to feel again? I didn't know, but that and many other questions went through my head as I frantically searched for the body with my fraternity ring on a finger.

"Finally I went into an isolation room where a body lay underneath sheets. The only thing visible was a hand with a black onyx ring on the finger. At that point I realized I had been flying around in a state of denial. I was dead—that was obvious—and I was outside of my body looking in. I began to weep and weep hard. I didn't know what to make of everything, but I did know that my body was no longer alive.

"As I wept the room became brighter, and then brighter and brighter, until it seemed as though a million welding torches were going off around me.

"I continued to weep. Then three things happened at the very same time. Something very deep in my spiritual being—not the corpse lying in the bed—said, 'Stand up! You are in the presence of the son of God!' Then, at the same instant, a magnificent being appeared, the most amazing I had ever met. The hospital walls around me disappeared, and I saw every little minute detail in my life, from my own C-section birth to my twentieth year up until the time I was pronounced dead. And I mean that I saw everything, and saw it in seconds.

"The being began to ask the question: 'What have you done with your life?' Well, I'm an Eagle Scout, I said. 'Yes, but that only glorified you.'

"I was stunned because I hadn't spoken, which means the be-ing had read my mind. To me that meant there is no hypocrisy because we can all read each other's thoughts, so you can't say one thing and mean another.

"At this point that meant there was no misunderstanding what he meant when he said I had only glorified myself. But de-spite that, he totally loved and accepted me.

"The next thing that happened was that Christ told me to come over and sit next to him. For a few moments he opened the heavenly realm to me so I could see it. But rather than let me be drawn into it, he pulled me back into this little room where I re-turned to my body."

When Ritchie finished talking, a number of hands went up and the questions began to flow. As they did, Ritchie passed around a death certificate from Camp Barkeley that was signed by Donald G. Francie, the doctor in charge when Ritchie died for the first time in his life.

To say I was hooked on death was an understatement. To deal with the great mind-body questions in a classroom was interest-ing but purely intellectual when compared to actually meeting someone who could prove he had left his body and traveled hun-dreds of miles.

Did I say "prove"? Yes, I did. As we looked at Ritchie's death certificate, the man for whom it had been made out told us that a year later he retraced the route of his out-of-body flight to find the diner in the small town where he had landed.

On this trip he was with some friends who all knew that Ritchie had never been to Vicksburg, Mississippi. As they drove through town, Ritchie made the announcement that if they turned at the next street and went down a block or two, they would come to a white diner on the corner of the street.

"You've never been here, George," said the friend who was driving.

"Not in my body," said Ritchie.

The driver turned quickly, and in two blocks they pulled up next to a white diner, the one Ritchie said he had visited during the out-of-body experience he had when he died.

Some of the medical staff at UVA once tried to hypnotize Ritchie to see if they could make him remember the experience of being almost dead. They got more than they asked for. As the doctors began to put him under, Ritchie went into heart failure, complete with distended neck veins and pain in his left arm. The doctor performing the hypnosis immediately terminated the treatment.

Ritchie at times had a direct line to God, he said. He felt the experience of returning from the dead had given that to him.

Ritchie said that one night an elderly patient called him and asked him to come to her house because her husband had died. Ritchie got to the house and found that the woman's husband was indeed lying in bed lifeless, without a heartbeat.

As he began to cover the man's face Ritchie heard a voice in his head say, "Tell him to get up!" Not one to argue with God, Ritchie stepped back and said loudly, "Get up!" The man's eyes opened and he stood up, said Ritchie. He lived several months longer and then expired for good.

Another time Ritchie and his wife Margarite were lost in their car in Washington, D.C. Ritchie pulled over to look at a map and happened to look up as a young man on the sidewalk passed the car. Once again a voice went off in Ritchie's head, telling him, "That young man is going to commit a murder!"

Ritchie told his wife what he had heard and then jumped out of the car to chase the young man down. "Excuse me," Ritchie said to the surprised pedestrian.

Unabashedly, Ritchie recounted the story for the puzzled man. "So are you on your way to murder someone?"

"Yes," said the young man, who felt he had been wronged by an acquaintance and was on his way to settle the score. The two talked for several minutes until Ritchie felt that it was safe for the man to go.

Ritchie said that he didn't feel that he was in any danger chasing down a stranger with such an unlikely message. "I had no doubt it was the voice of God, and he wouldn't steer me wrong."

Hearing Ritchie's story of death and rebirth had a major impact on me. I associated his story with those told by Socrates. To me, Ritchie was a modern-day soldier of Ur. As far as I knew, George Ritchie was the only living person to have gone through such an experience. I didn't make the inference that there must be more people like Ritchie—indeed, many more people like him. Not until a few years later would I find out how wrong I was to think of this experience as unique.

After the room cleared out, I approached Ritchie. Because my father had frequent bouts of anger for seemingly no reason, I often had difficulty talking to adult males. But Ritchie's voice was kind and his demeanor so easy that I immediately felt at ease with him. I told him that his story clearly answered the mind-body question of interest to anyone who had ever studied philosophy.

"For you, there is no question about whether the mind and body coexist," I said.

"None whatsoever," he said. "For me, the brain is like a receiver and is not the cause of consciousness. It's just receiving consciousness from somewhere else."

Ritchie and I became fast friends. I think he determined early on that he had met his intellectual match in me. I was well read, and he, though not as well read, was "well lived." He shared his life experiences freely and took me under his wing, talking to me about the diseases and disorders he dealt with as the student body psychiatrist.

I remember one time asking him if any of his student patients had ever related an experience like his own. He thought a moment. "When I speak to large groups, several people always come up afterward and tell me about similar experiences," he declared.

Unfortunately, Ritchie never wrote down those experiences that were shared with him. Nor did he save them when they arrived in the mail. One time he wrote an article for *Guideposts* magazine and received "a batch" of letters from people who had had the same sort of experience. They were writing for help, said Ritchie, and there were so many of them that there was no way he could reasonably be expected to respond to them.

Eventually his wife threw them in the trash when she was cleaning the house.

When my research garnered so much attention years later that I received a book contract, Ritchie shook his head over the loss of all that great data. "I could have been you," he said.

I had many great official professors at UVA, but the best of the unofficial ones was George Ritchie. We met at least once a week for coffee (although I drank Coca-Cola) and talked extensively about the human mind. It was as a result of these sessions that I became more and more interested in psychiatry as a profession. I began to see psychiatry as a practical application of philosophy, given that so many of the issues brought to the psychiatrist's couch stem from the same "meaning of life" questions posed by philosophers.

Ritchie agreed with me on that.

"It doesn't matter if you are Albert Einstein or a day laborer in Egypt," said Ritchie. "All people have the same questions about life and death, and so far no one has answered them in a satisfactory way. So as we go along, century after century, mankind still wants to know why we are here and what happens when we're not."

I began to talk to my professors and family about psychiatry and the possibility of practicing it as a profession. Most everyone I spoke to was encouraging, including my father, who confessed to me that he had considered psychiatry himself before deciding instead on general surgery.

I have to say, I was surprised by that announcement. My father was perfectly suited to be a general surgeon and, to my way of thinking, didn't have the patience to be in the "talking arts." The age-old description of a surgeon was written for my father: "To be great, a surgeon must have a fierce determination to be the leader in his field. He must have a driving ego, a hunger beyond money. He must have a passion for perfectionism."

For my father to believe as Ritchie did that "the best medical book you'll ever read is the patients themselves" was in no way possible.

Raymond Moody Sr. was in no way a people person.

CHAPTER SIX

I graduated from UVA four years later with a doctorate in philosophy. These years were a blur of studying, reading, frequent meetings with professors, and student teaching. By the time I graduated I was married to Louise Lamback, a beautiful girl who looked at me and saw her future.

I had been deep in study for years, but the death experience of George Ritchie continuously came up in my readings, especially those that related to ancient Greece. In fact, the Greeks were so comfortable with the subject that they actually wrote satires about it. Lucian of Samsota wrote a parody of a dinner party where people are talking about their supernatural experiences. One of the guests speaks about being so sick at the party that he actually gets out of his body, a feat that stuns the assembled diners.

Still, for some reason I thought that George Ritchie was the only living person who had gone through such an interesting experience at death and that all of the others could only be found in ancient Greece. I didn't make the inference that there could be more people out there who were just like Ritchie—but chose to remain silent about their experience.

A couple of things happened during my doctorate program that should have indicated to me that things were not normal in my body. One was that I began to have the sensation that color was disappearing from my vision. This first happened when we were going to paint the living room of our rental house and Louise brought home an entire can of bright red paint. She asked what I thought of the color, and I said that it looked fine, but in truth I couldn't tell what color it was. The entire can just looked sort of gray to me.

Another thing I should have taken notice of was my body temperature. Over the years at UVA I had begun to feel colder and colder. In the winter, when the classrooms were baking from the school's overly efficient heaters, I kept on the woolen clothing I wore outdoors. I wore a jacket even when summer came around and then sometimes found myself shivering in class.

The most obvious warning sign occurred on graduation day in June 1969. It was a sweltering day, and the graduation ceremony was being held outside. The combination of heat, humidity, and sizzling sun was causing the lightly dressed people around us to collapse from heat prostration. I, on the other hand, was wearing a heavy tweed jacket with a dress shirt and tie and not sweating at all. *What's wrong with these people?* I thought, never thinking that there was something wrong with me.

. . .

Before graduating from UVA, I was hired by East Carolina University to teach philosophy. I was given a dream job by the head of the small department. My duties were to teach basic philosophy with an emphasis on Plato. That meant that I would deal with a variety of the topics—justice, knowledge, wisdom, ethics, logic, mathematics, rhetoric, the afterlife—that lay the foundations of Western philosophy and science.

I was thrilled to spend my days in a classroom lecturing to a dozen or so students whose assignment was to read the dialogues of Plato and be prepared to discuss them in class. I had a few students who fell asleep in class or who expressed a variety of excuses for not completing their reading assignments, but I accepted the fact that some students were not interested in the origins of Western thought or were just not cut out for the questioning nature it takes to be in a philosophy class, let alone be a philosopher.

Some students, however, were extremely interested in the works of Plato, and some even demanded to go further than I expected to go. One of those students was a young man I'll call Ross.

Ross was such a mess that I could hardly keep my eyes off of him during class. He had been in an automobile accident, and his arms were severely burned and covered with scars. I assumed that he was unable to raise them as high as his head because his dark hair had not been adequately combed for some time and was a mass of cowlicks that stuck out in different directions. In the beginning of the semester he had been fairly enthusiastic about the class, but after a few weeks he fell quiet and at times was somewhat surly. He became exasperated at what we were studying and more than once closed his book and used it as a pillow.

One day after class he waited until the room cleared and then limped to the teacher's desk where I was sitting. He looked both nervous and agitated when I looked up.

"Dr. Moody, I wish we could talk about something else in this class," he said.

"What do you have in mind, Ross?" I asked.

"How about life after death?" he said, somewhat sarcastically. "Isn't that what *philosophy* is really all about?"

"Why do you want to talk about that?" I asked.

"Because about a year ago I was in a bad accident, and my doctors said I died. And I had an experience that has totally changed my life, but I haven't had anybody to talk about it with."

My eyes opened wide and my heart began to race. *Was this an experience like George Ritchie's?* I asked myself. *Have I found another one?*

I closed my books and invited Ross back to my office. He limped down the hall and into my modest workplace. Next to him on top of a metal file cabinet was a stack of Donald Duck and Uncle Scrooge comics. Ross looked at me slightly askance and shrugged. "I'm a big fan," I said. The comic books were an icebreaker for Ross. He smiled slightly—the first smile I had seen from him all semester—and began telling me a story that was very similar to those of the soldier of Ur and Dr. Ritchie.

"I was in a bad car accident on the freeway north of town. I hit a car that was parked on the side of the road and went from going sixty miles per hour to almost zero in a split second. I had my seat belt on, so I stayed in the car, but my arms were broken by the steering wheel, my head hit the window and shattered it, and a flash fire burned my arms terribly.

"When the ambulance arrived, the emergency team came right over and began checking me. One of them stepped back and said, "I'm not finding a pulse." Then he went back to my body and kept looking.

"I couldn't tell what was happening because I was over the accident and looking down at my body. I could see the emergency workers trying to untangle me from the steering wheel, and I could still tell that they didn't know if I was alive or dead.

"All of a sudden I could see a tunnel open that was made of light. It pulled me inside of it, and out of the light came a man made of light that I think was Jesus.

"He let me see my entire life from the beginning to this moment. This image of my life came right out of a wall of light and looked like a television that I could actually step into if I had wanted.

"There was an end to the images, and when that happened I went high above the wreck site and could see cities of light. I have no idea what cities they were."

Ross told me his story in a very matter-of-fact way. It wasn't until I asked him what the impact on him had been that he became emotional.

"It was a terrible experience, but at the same time a good one too," he said. "I don't know if I'll ever recover from this accident, but I know that what happened has changed my life forever. I know there's a life after death, and I know that love is very important. But I want to know if there are more people like me who've had this experience. That's why I took your *philosophy* class, because I want to know what this means."

The emphasis Ross put on the word "philosophy" told me that my class had been a disappointment for him up to this point. I vowed to deal with the issue of the afterlife in our next class.

When Ross left my office, I was stunned. *What are the statistical chances that Raymond Moody would hear the only two cases that exist in the world and hear those within a four-year period?* I asked myself. The answer was, of course, no chance at all. I began to wonder just how prevalent these experiences were, and just what they meant. I took out a notebook and began to write questions about these "death experiences" that I felt needed answering:

Are people who have these experiences truly dead?

Do the same events happen to everyone?

If so, do these events happen in the same pattern with everyone, or can they happen in any order?

When people leave their body, do they see events that they can recall later that would prove they actually left their body?

Do people on the "other side" tell them stories or events related to their own life that they had never heard before then?

Does having this experience change people's life upon their return?

Does a person who has this experience bring back any "special powers"?

Is it possible that these events change the clinical definition of death?

Are these events proof of life after life?

I immediately shifted gears and changed the way I taught the class. I made Plato interactive by having the students read the *Phaedo,* a work that deals largely with his views of the afterlife.

Then, when we reached the part where Plato talks about being out of body, I would stop and say, "You know, I'm very interested in what might happen to people between life and death. If anyone has a story about a relative or even themselves actually leaving their body during an illness or accident, I would very much like to hear it."

Students immediately sought me out. It was as though these events had haunted them for years and now they had a chance to talk to someone who would not be judgmental or think they were crazy.

I did not tape-record these early stories, but I remember them nonetheless. One was from a young woman who knocked on my office door and shyly began to tell me about her father, who'd had a heart attack when she was a child. When he returned from the hospital, he told her in secret that he had watched her and her mother stand over his body and not know what to do. When they finally called the hospital and he was loaded into the ambulance, he said he had followed above the vehicle all the way to the hospital, where he was able to see doctors prep him for emergency bypass surgery.

"He wanted me to know what had happened to him, but he asked me not to tell anyone because they might think he was crazy," she told me. "So I have kept it to myself until now."

A young man with a blond crew cut came in to tell me about being run over by a car when he was a little boy. He hadn't been injured, he said, but as the car passed over him he could see every nut and bolt underneath the car so clearly that it was as though the car was barely moving.

As well as seeing the bottom of the car in detail, the young man witnessed his entire young life passing before him in a way that he said was "very bizarre."

"Dr. Moody, I not only saw everything that had ever happened to me, I also felt the emotions of everything in my life," he said. "Even though it happened fifteen years ago, it has never left my mind. It is like it happened yesterday."

Soon my house became a gathering point for students who wanted to discuss these mysterious experiences. Then many adults came to tell their stories. A dentist in his fifties came to the house one time and said he had heard about the stories I was collecting from a friend of his son's. He told me that he had been in an auto wreck years earlier and had left his body before the ambulance arrived and again later when he was in surgery. It was on the operating table that he'd had a very intense experience with "this light." I turned on the tape recorder as he told the story:

"I knew I was dying and that there was nothing I could do about it, because no one could hear me. . . . I was out of my body, there's no doubt about it, because I could see my own body there on the operating room table. My soul was out! All this made me feel very bad at first, but then this really bright light came. It did seem that it was a little dim at first, but then it was this huge beam. It was just a tremendous amount of light, nothing like a big bright flashlight, it was just too much light. And it gave off heat to me: I felt a warm sensation.

"It was a bright yellowish white—more white. It was tremendously bright; I just can't describe it. It seemed that it covered everything, yet it didn't prevent me from seeing everything around me—the operating room, the doctors and nurses, everything. I could see clearly, and it wasn't blinding.

"At first, when the light came, I wasn't sure what was happening, but then it asked, it kind of asked me if I was ready to die. It was like talking to a person, but a person wasn't there. The light's what was talking to me, but in a voice.

"Now I think that the voice that was talking to me actually realized that I wasn't ready to die. You know, it was just kind of testing me more than anything else. Yet, from the moment the light spoke to me, I felt really good—secure and loved. The love that came from it is just unimaginable, indescribable. It was a fun person to be with! And it had a sense of humor too—definitely."

In short order, I tape-recorded eight mysterious experiences that happened at the point of death.

Word about what I was doing got out quickly in the small town of Greenville, South Carolina. A student spoke to a friend of his who was a local newspaper reporter, who did a short article about the philosophy teacher who was asking students for accounts of experiences at the point of death.

After the article came out, I expected some problems from the local churches, whose members I thought would see my interest in these experiences as an affront to religion. But I was surprised. The first organization to ask me to speak about my findings was the Jarvis Memorial United Methodist Church. I was invited to its Wednesday night potluck supper by Karl Fazer, the assistant provost of East Carolina University and a former Marine colonel.

I had become a good public speaker, but I was still nervous that night as I faced several dozen people who were, well, religious enough to spend Wednesday night in a church.

I told the congregation about Plato and about Dr. Ritchie and then about the student who wanted to tell me about the accident that seemed to take him to a different world. I wondered out loud if there were some stories in this very room like the ones I was about to play on the tape recorder.

Then I hit the play button.

The eating in the room stopped as the congregants put down their forks and listened. I could see that Colonel Fazer was getting agitated by what he was hearing, but I couldn't tell if he was aghast or amazed.

He stood up from his place at the front table and walked to the tape recorder. He bent at the waist and put his ear to the speaker for a long enough time that I began to get nervous. Then he straightened up and said, "This is real! These people aren't making it up! This is real!"

I tried to appear unmoved, the way I thought a truly objective researcher should look. But I couldn't. I began to smile and nod my head at the raw emotion that came from Colonel Fazer.

I knew I was on to something big.

CHAPTER SEVEN

~

You can guide your life to a certain extent, and then, if you are lucky, serendipity takes over. It leads you down a path that you would not have considered an option. Once you've experienced that path, though, you become comfortable with it and know that it is the path you should have chosen all along.

That is what happened to me in studying these as-of-yet-unnamed experiences. I was constantly approached by people who wanted to tell me their story or the story of a loved one. For example, one day in downtown Greenville I was approached by a woman who had seen me at the church where I spoke and wanted to tell me the story of what had happened to her husband when he had his heart attack.

"After my husband's heart attack, I knew right away that something was different. I asked him if the medicine was affecting him, and he said that it went way beyond that. He said when his heart stopped, the floor seemed to go out from under him and he was up in the air watching the ambulance attendants take him away, and then later he watched as the doctors put a tube in his arm and tried to get his heart started. He said he saw his mother too. She had died ten years ago but was a great comfort for him while he was up there."

On another occasion a man stopped me on campus and asked if I was that "Dr. Death" he had read about. He said he had fallen from a ladder while working on his home and landed on his head.

"I lay there for several minutes before I was found. At first everything was black, like I was in a closet. Then the roof seemed to open up, and I went up this spiral tunnel and into a bright light. It was great and I didn't want to wake up. But here I am."

I was studying for medical school entrance exams at the time, as well as teaching and collecting stories. A pattern was beginning to emerge in these stories, but I felt I needed to see many more before drawing any conclusions. At this point I just called them "afterlife stories" because that seemed to encompass the popular perception of what they were. As a result, some of the students, like the man who had told me his story about falling off a ladder, began to call me "Dr. Death"—not a particularly endearing nickname to pin on someone who was hoping to make it into medical school.

Despite that moniker, I was accepted into the Medical College of Georgia in 1972. Several of my friends from Macon had gone there and were now upperclassmen. They knew of the research I was doing and told the professors of my work.

Having it generally known at the medical school that I was studying these afterlife experiences made me cautious. I was concerned that I would face criticism for studying experiences like these in an institution dedicated to medicine, not metaphysics. But that concern disappeared as I discovered that the staff was very interested in what I was studying and what I had to say about it.

The first member of the medical staff to show interest in my work was Claude Starr Wright, my hematology professor. A few years earlier he had resuscitated a fellow doctor and friend who nearly died of a heart attack. When the man revived, he looked up in anger at Wright and said, "Next time this happens let me die!"

The doctor went on to tell him of an experience that was painless, peaceful, and filled with the promise of a life after life.

"Life is like imprisonment," he told his fellow MD a few days later. "In this state we just can't understand what prisons these bodies are. Death is a release—like an escape from prison. That's the best thing I can think of to compare it to."

Wright, who had heard about a few more of these experiences since he saved his doctor friend, said to me, "I would like to know what these experiences are all about." He thought it was good that someone had come into the medical school with a fresh idea about what should be studied.

Other doctors encouraged me too. Russ Moores, another hematology professor, had heard these afterlife stories from a number of patients as well as from other doctors, and he too wanted to see them studied. "We don't know what the implications of these experiences are, and we need to know that," he said. "This could be a whole new field, and up to now it has been ignored."

During my first couple of weeks I heard eight afterlife stories from the teaching staff, about half of which were experiences they'd had themselves.

Seven months after starting medical school, I was invited to speak before the Milton Anthony Medical Society about the phenomenology of what I had come to call "the near-death experience." I called it the near-death experience because those who had it were not technically dead but were very close to it. And yes, this definition included those who had suffered cardiac arrest. They were as close as they could be to death, yet were not there yet. "Death is the cessation of all bodily functions," I said to the fifty or so doctors who filled the rotunda. "At least all bodily functions we know of."

My years of teaching had erased my fear of public speaking, but on this day I had to admit that my hands were perspiring as I addressed the common elements in about twenty of my case studies.

When I finished my talk, a polite round of applause was followed by one of the doctors holding up his hand. An Amish doctor who taught anatomy at the medical college, he was a gruff man who liked to challenge students in class, and he was about to challenge me now.

"Dr. Moody, I have been in medicine for many years now. Why haven't I heard of this before?"

I was ready to throw his question out to the audience when his wife held up her hand and began speaking.

"Don't you remember our friend Janet telling us about how this happened to her?" she asked. "Janet had an experience just like the one you've described here."

A hearty laugh arose from the assembled doctors. The ice was broken, and the secret stories they had never before shared came pouring out. I interviewed at least two of the doctors who told their story that day, adding their commentary to the near-death experience archive I was collecting.

Early in my second year of medical school I was invited to speak at the Bibb County Medical Association, where a reporter from the *Macon News and Telegram* was in attendance. Based on what she heard that day, she wrote an article that brought me attention in the community and even more case studies.

Then everything quickly changed for me. A reporter from the *Atlanta Constitution* came to interview me after reading the article in the Macon paper. By now I had examined several dozen of these experiences and broken them down into their component parts: the out-of-body experience, the sensation of traveling through a tunnel, seeing and/or communicating with dead relatives, and so on.

The reporter spent a lot of time with me making sure he got it right. What came out was a long and honest piece about what I was calling the near-death experience.

When the article was published, I suddenly became the most famous medical student in Georgia. Even my father was proud. He had been quiet about my research until the *Constitution* article came out. Now he was showing that article to his colleagues and patients, clearly thrilled that his son had gotten some ink.

It was during this very heady period that I received a call from John Egle, an editor for Ballantine Books in New York City. Egle said that he had read the newspaper article and felt the subject of near-death experiences would make a very popular book. Would I, he asked, allow him to pay a visit?

I was now in my third year of medical school and as busy as I could ever be. In addition to studying for my degree and collecting what was now an almost steady stream of near-death experience stories from people, Louise was pregnant with our first child, who was due to be born in only a few months. Did I have time to see him?

"Of course I'll see you, John," I said. "Come on down."

A few days later John Egle showed up. A tall thin man with curly brown hair, he was born exactly ten years earlier than I was, on June 3o, 1934. He was ebullient about all of his projects, but the prospect of getting a book about the near-death experience into the marketplace had his full attention and enthusiasm.

Egle spent a lot of time reading my lectures and listening to the audiotapes I had made of the individuals as they described their experiences. At the end of the day Egle ran his hands through his hair and said, "Wow."

We spoke for a while about the material and whether I believed that it represented proof positive of life after death. I told him that I didn't believe it did, but that I did think the near-death experience was at least a gateway experience that took a person right up to the point of no return. What happened after that, no one can know, I said to Egle. That would be the point of true death.

Egle nodded his head somberly. I had already found that people insisted on bringing the same somber demeanor to this subject as they would have while sitting in a funeral parlor waiting for the service to begin. I didn't know whether they thought I somehow required that the subject be treated this way or if they just saw death as a somber subject. Whatever the case, since I saw the results of my research as some of the best news ever for those concerned that death was the end of all consciousness, I tried to put some levity into our conversation.

"So the message here is to not be so serious about death anymore," I said to John. "At least the ride to the pearly gates is pretty cool."

Egle nodded seriously for a moment until he realized I was putting him on. Then he broke a smile.

Assuring me that "this is going to be a big book," Egle asked me what title I had in mind. "Life After Life," I said. Egle left that day promising that he would talk to the top editor, Ian Ballantine, as soon as possible about making an offer. In a couple of days he called back to tell me that Ballantine had agreed to offer a $1,000 advance against royalties. In March I received a contract from Ballantine and a letter congratulating me for developing such a fine concept for a book. The contract gave me only six months to turn in a completed manuscript.

I was thrilled. I was going to be a book author.

CHAPTER EIGHT

~

When I started writing about life after death, I had Plato in mind. He was the founder of academia, the man who formed the institution that gave people MDs and PhDs and the like. If the founder of academia thought that life after death was mankind's most important question, surely anybody who comes out of that academic system needs to listen very carefully to what he had to say about it.

Plato set up the argument for the life-after-death question by making the most important statement anybody has ever made about the methodology of studying the afterlife. In the *Phaedo* he makes two important points:

- There always has to be a narrative element in studying the afterlife because that is how people connect with concepts of living beyond physical death.

- There also has to be a conceptual means of reasoning—a logic—that can take the truth-seeker beyond just stories and into the stream of objective truth.

He emphasizes that when we talk about the afterlife we are not using literal language. Rather, we are speaking words of consolation for people who are afraid of death. Plato also writes that talking about the afterlife is a form of incantation or "magic words."

"We ought to repeat them to ourselves over and over to arm ourselves against the vicissitudes of life," he says.

Oddly, these comments inspired me to press on with the book. I was developing a form of logic that would allow sound reasoning about an afterlife. In short, I wanted to go beyond Plato. But that would culminate later, I realized, if ever at all.

I quickly jotted down a note, the essence of which would eventually be included in the beginning of *Life After Life*: "I want to assure my fellow philosophers that I'm not under the delusion that I have proven an afterlife. . . . And furthermore, for reasons I shall much later explain, I don't even think that such a proof is currently possible."

By writing this, I was hoping that the reader would see all of the difficulties in researching this topic and appreciate the brain power that has gone into its examination over the centuries.

Later, those comments were taken out of the book by the editor, who insisted that readers would think I was "taking it all back" if it were left in. I fumed about that editorial decision for some time, but in retrospect I believe that removing those sentences was the right thing to do. Had I left them in, I would have been pushing too many contrary thoughts into the book, including ones that needed to be dealt with by those who wanted to study the afterlife more deeply.

I saw this book as a work that could go beyond just telling stories of people who almost died to examine phenomenology, a description of the characteristics of a specific type of experience. By focusing the work on the phenomenology of the near-death experience, I would be breaking these amazing events into their component parts, thereby making them easier to research. The first step in the process was to dissect all of the case studies and outline the different traits present in almost all of these experiences. As I wrote:

> Despite the striking similarities among various accounts, no two of them are precisely identical (though a few come remarkably close to it).
>
> I have found no one person who reports every single component of the composite experience. Very many have reported most of them (that is, eight or more of the fifteen or so) and a few have reported up to twelve.
>
> There is no one element of the composite experience which every single person has reported to me, which crops up in every narrative. Nonetheless, a few of these elements come fairly close to being universal.
>
> How far into the hypothetical complete experience a dying person gets seems to depend on whether the person actually underwent an apparent clinical death, and if so, on how long he or she was in this state. In general, persons who were "dead" seem to report more complex, complete experiences than those who only came close to death, and those who were "dead" for a longer time go deeper than those who were "dead" for a shorter time.
>
> I have talked to a few people who were pronounced dead, resuscitated, and came back reporting none of these

common elements. Indeed, they say they don't remember anything at all about their "deaths." Interestingly enough, I have talked with several persons who were actually adjudged clinically dead on separate occasions years apart, and reported experiencing nothing on one of the occasions, but having had quite involved experiences on the other.

I then presented all of the traits I had found of the phenomenon I called the near-death experience:

Ineffability: These experiences are virtually ineffable, or "inexpressible," because there are no words in our community of language to express consciousness at the point of death. That is why many people who've had NDEs [near-death experiences] say things like, "There are just no words to express what I am trying to say." This, of course, presents a problem because if they can't describe what's happened, they can't gain understanding from another person.

Hearing the News: Numerous people in the course of my research told of hearing their doctors or others pronounce them dead.

Feelings of Peace and Quiet: Many people described pleasant feelings and sensations during their experience, even after being pronounced dead. One man with a severe head injury and no detectable vital signs said that all pain vanished as he floated in a dark space and realized, "I must be dead."

The Noise: In many of the cases, people reported unusual auditory sensations, like a loud buzzing noise or a loud ring. Some found this noise to be quite pleasant while others found it to be extremely annoying.

The Dark Tunnel: People reported the sensation of being pulled very rapidly through a dark space, most often described as being a tunnel. For instance, in one case a man who "died" several times during burns and fall injuries said that he escaped into a "dark void" in which he floated and tumbled through space.

Out of the Body: During these experiences, usually after the tunnel experience, the people would have the sense of leaving their body and looking at themselves from a physical point outside of it. Some described it as being "the third person in the room," or like being "on a stage in a play." The experiences they had out of body were quite detailed and often involved an understanding that they were dead yet were observing their physical body. Many of the people described medical procedures and activity with such detail that there was little doubt on the part of attending physicians interviewed later that some kind of actual witnessing of events on the part of the comatose patient had occurred.

Meeting Others: Out-of-body experiences usually followed tunnel experiences and were usually followed by the meeting of other "spiritual beings" in their vicinity, beings who were there to ease them through their transition and into death, or to tell that that it wasn't their time to die.

The Being of Light: The most incredible common element that I found and the one that had the greatest effect on the individual is the encounter with a very bright light, one that is most often described as a "being of light." This being first appeared as a dim light and then became rapidly brighter until it reached an unearthly brilliance.

Often described as "Jesus," "God," or an "angel" by those with religious training, the light communicates with the individual (sometimes in a language they have never heard) often asking them if they are "ready to die," or what their accomplishments are.

The being of light does not ask these questions in a judgmental way. Rather it asks Socratic questions, ones aimed at acquiring information that can help the person proceed along a path of truth and self realization.

The light or being of light is described as "unimaginable" or "indescribable" as well as "funny," "pleasant," or "secure."

The Review: The probing questions of the being of light would often lead to a review of one's life, a moment of startling power during which a person's entire life was displayed before them in panoramic intensity. The review is extraordinarily rapid and in chronological order, and is incredibly vivid and real. Sometimes it is even described as "three-dimensional." Others describe it as "highly-charged" with emotions and even multi-dimensions in a way that the individual can understand the thoughts of everyone in the review.

The review is most often described as an educational effort on the part of the being of light, one aimed at individuals understanding themselves better.

The Border or Limit: In some of these cases, the person describes approaching a "border" or "limit," beyond which they will not return. This border is described variously as being water, a gray mist, a door, a fence across a field, or even a line or an imaginary line.

In one such case, a person was escorted to the line by the being of light and asked if he wanted to die. When he said he knew nothing about death, the being told him, "Come over this line and you will learn." When he did, he experienced "the most wonderful feeling" of peace, tranquility, and a vanishing of all worries.

Coming Back: Obviously, the individuals I talked with came back to their physical lives. Some resisted their return and wanted to stay in this afterlife state. Some reported return trips through the tunnel and back to their physical bodies. But when they did return, they had moods and feelings that lingered for a long time. Many were transformed and reported becoming "better" people.

Telling Others: The people I spoke to were normal people with functioning, well-balanced personalities. Yet because they were afraid of being labeled as delusional or mentally ill, these people often chose to remain silent about their experience or only relate it to someone very close to them. Because there was no common language in which to express their experience, they chose to keep it to themselves so no one would think they had become mentally unbalanced as a result of their brush with death.

It wasn't until many individuals heard of the research I was doing that they felt comfortable enough to relate their experience to others. I was frequently thanked by these long-silent NDEers, who would say, "Thank you for your work. Now I know I'm not crazy."

Effects on Lives: Despite the desire of most of these individuals to remain quiet about their experience, the effect of these experiences on their lives was profound and noticeable. Many told me their lives had broadened and deepened through these experiences, that they had become more reflective of life and more gentle with those around them. Their vision left them with new goals, new moral principles, and a renewed determination to live in accordance with them.

New Views of Death: In the end they all reported new views about death. They no longer feared death yet many had the sense that they had a lot of personal growth to attend to before leaving their physical life. They also came to believe that there is no "reward and punishment" model of the afterlife. Rather, the being of light made their sinful deeds obvious to them and made it clear that life was a learning process, not a platform for later judgment.

Developing these component parts was the most important part of the book. No one had ever studied these experiences, and indeed there wasn't even a name for them—near-death experiences—until I began my studies. But the component parts were most important because they gave doctors and medical researchers a way to communicate with those who had had near-death experiences. Before my work, medical personnel might have dismissed these important events in a person's life as no more than a bad dream or false memory. But now doctors and patients alike would have a reference point from which to begin a discussion about a patient's near-death experience.

Given that this phenomenon had never been seriously examined by modern medicine, I was careful to include some form of corroboration from the medical community for these experiences. Without that, I feared that *Life After Life* might be considered the work of a New Ager or a religious zealot, neither of which came close to describing my orientation.

At the end of the chapter about the traits of the near-death experience, I added a section entitled, simply, "Corroboration." I focused on the most obvious of the traits, the out-of-body experience. "Many persons report being out of their bodies for extended periods and witnessing many events in the physical world during the interlude," I wrote. "Can any of these reports be checked out with other witnesses who were known to be present, or with later confirming events, and thus be corroborated?"

To answer that question, I pointed out that many doctors had told me that they were "utterly baffled" at how a patient with no medical knowledge could describe the details of the resuscitation attempts even though the patient was thought to be dead at the time.

Some individuals reported leaving the hospital room where their physical body lay and traveling into the waiting room to be with frightened family members. These patients later surprised their doctors by recalling events and conversations that they could not have possibly been witness to if they had not been present.

I related one story in which a girl left her dying body and found her older sister crying in another room, saying, "Oh, Kathy, please don't die, please don't die." The older sister was baffled when Kathy later told her where she had been and what she was saying.

I then provided two small case studies. In one of them, a pa-

tient told his doctor about medical procedures he should not have
been able to see during his cardiac arrest:

> After it was all over, the doctor told me that I had a really
> bad time, and I said, "Yeah, I know." He said, "Well, how do
> you know?" and I said, "I can tell you everything that hap-
> pened." He didn't believe me, so I told him the whole story,
> from the time I stopped breathing until the time I was kind
> of coming around. He was really shocked to know that I
> knew everything that had happened. He didn't know quite
> what to say, but he came in several times to ask me different
> things about it.

If there was a weak spot in my research, it was probably in
this corroboration section, but I knew that more such evidence
would come with time. Still, even addressing the subject with
the slim amount of material I had would make it clear that these
experiences had some kind of validation with witnesses who
were present.

I decided to skip the sensationalist writing that the copious
use of adjectives would have afforded me, opting instead to write
the book in an almost flat tone. I figured that the material itself
was sensational enough to carry the day. Any attempt by me to
amp it up would demean not only my credibility but also that of
the brave people who had put their trust in me to tell their story
in an uncompromising way.

I wrote the book over the summer of 1974. Dr. Moores offered to
let me do it as a summer school class for extra credit if I would let

him listen to the tape recordings of my interviews. It seemed like a fair trade to me. I settled into a routine of writing, and in about two months *Life After Life* was complete.

"Well, you can rest now, you've done it," said Egle when I delivered the manuscript.

Egle was now living on Georgia's St. Simons Island, where he had moved as part of a grand experiment concocted by the venerable Ian Ballantine himself, who had decided to open several small branches of his company around the country to make sure they captured any good local books that might otherwise slip through the net. The experiment proved to be a failure, and now Ballantine had decided to either close these branch offices or turn them over to the individual book editors. Egle decided to keep operating his little publishing company, which was called Mockingbird Press.

All of which does little to explain why my book manuscript sat on a shelf in New York for a full year before Egle called me with the disheartening news that the editor who had taken it over wanted me to "novelize" it.

"That's not going to happen!" I said to Egle, who adamantly agreed with me.

Egle pointed out to me that a year had passed without publication and therefore the contract with Ballantine had lapsed. That meant, said Egle, that the completed manuscript was mine. I could, he said, take it to another publisher.

"John, I want you to publish it," I said. "This was your project to begin with, and you obviously have a passion for this. Please do it!"

A few days later Egle wrote a letter to Ballantine pointing out that the contract on *Life After Life* had lapsed and that Dr. Moody wanted to make other arrangements for its publication. Ballantine responded quickly, saying that they would gladly relinquish the rights and assuring me that the $1,000 advance did not have to be paid back.

I was delighted to be free of my contract, delighted to be free of pressure to fictionalize the rawest truth I had ever heard, and delighted to be published by John Egle's little company, Mockingbird Press.

Egle was optimistic too.

"This book is going to be big," he said.

"How big?" I asked.

"I'll bet it sells as many as ten thousand copies."

I had stars in my eyes at the thought of ten thousand people reading my book.

When I received the galley proofs of *Life After Life* in November 1975, I realized that I had not yet dedicated the book to anyone. I considered dedicating it to my father, but he had not been supportive of my efforts to research this topic any more than he had been supportive of any of my areas of interest.

I decided instead to dedicate it to Dr. George Ritchie, who had been like a mentor to me in studying and discussing the issues of life after life.

I called Ritchie and asked his permission to dedicate the book to him.

"I appreciate that," said Ritchie. "But I would rather you dedicate it to Jesus Christ because he is the one who gave me this experience."

This presented a true dilemma to me. I didn't want the book to seem aimed at a Christian audience, which a dedication to Christ would certainly have done. I wanted to stay neutral on the question of religion. I felt that the notion of life after life extends to all people, even atheists. I didn't want anyone to think that I came at this subject with a religious bias.

Finally we agreed on a dedication that was acceptable to all:

> To George Ritchie, MD, and through him
> to the One whom he suggested.

Life After Life went to press.

CHAPTER NINE

The first inkling that *Life After Life* was going to be a huge success came from my friend John Ouzts. He was listening to Europe on his shortwave radio when he heard a long news report coming from Dublin radio that spoke glowingly about the book.

"I think you're sitting on a rocket," said Ouzts. "This book is getting attention around the world."

He was right. For reasons that can only be explained in retrospect, *Life After Life* climbed onto every bestseller list in the world, where it stayed for more than three years. Why this took place can be answered in one word: vacuum. Up to this point the subject had been considered one that belonged to the world of religion, and therefore it had received little if any examination by medical science. Hence, there was no real scientific examination of the possibility of life after life.

Life After Life was a book that even an atheist could appreciate. It did not bring God or religion into the discussion—not really. Rather, it defined and explored a series of events that take place— that have always taken place—at the point of death. Suddenly there was research that approached the subject of death in a methodical and measured way. With the publication of this book, the medical establishment was free to talk about the process of death and dying without having to allude to religious beliefs. With *Life After Life*, doctors and nurses now had talking points to help them discuss death with the terminally ill and their families. Many in the medical field were relieved by the book's appearance. They had heard these stories from their own patients and didn't know that they represented a universal phenomenon. Now they did, and the popularity of the book not only gave them permission to discuss its content but almost demanded it.

Overnight the phrase "near-death experience" came into the world's lexicon. In no time at all I was hearing phrases like "out of body" and "tunnel experience" and "being of light" on television and radio. Newspapers, comic strips, and late-night talk shows prominently mentioned near-death experiences, and they even became a punch line for comedians. It was as though I had opened a secret room and everyone wanted what was inside.

My life changed abruptly. I was still in medical school, my third year, but I was no longer treated strictly as a student. As my book climbed the bestseller list, my status rose. Professors often deferred to me in class. Nurses whispered when I passed.

When I finished my surgical rotation, for example, I had to take an oral examination, a particularly nerve-wracking form of testing in which I would have to present all of my surgical cases to a professor who would question me in harsh detail. Or so it was supposed to be. ——

For me it was different. I was greeted by a smiling professor who had looked at my cases the day before and selected one to talk about, a woman who had presented with a lipoma. A benign tumor made from fat, a lipoma is more unsightly than dangerous. As I recall, the patient had asked for hers to be removed because it showed as a lump on her back that was visible under her dress.

"Dr. Moody, tell me about the malignant potentiality of a lipoma," the professor asked.

I shrugged. "Almost nil," I said. "It's just a ball of adipose tissue."

"Excellent," he said. "Dr. Moody, I deal with a lot of terminally ill patients, and I am so grateful for your work. Now I know how to answer their questions. It's a relief for them to feel the hope that I felt after reading your book."

The rest of my oral examination in surgery was spent talking about near-death experiences and the direction I would take next in this new field, which had already become known as "near-death studies."

The professor's question was a good one: What new direction would I take in near-death studies? The success of the book had set me on a course over which I had little control. Market forces were pushing me deeper into my own field of near-death studies. As a professor once said to me, "Raymond, you have no choice but to continue with near-death studies. We all follow the path of least resistance, which is the direction in which our work is accepted the most."

I knew exactly what he meant. Before I began my near-death studies, I was the death of a party. Literally. When asked at a party what I was working on, eyes would glaze over when I said that I was studying Godel's theorem or some other abstruse philosophical precept. Later, though, when it became known that I was studying near-death experiences, people couldn't get enough of me and my work. They would gather around to hear about the latest case study or to ask questions about these visions of the afterlife.

This deep interest in my work from all corners of life helped keep me on the path of discovery. But in truth, I didn't need a lot of help to stay focused. By the time I had interviewed thirty or forty of these individuals, I knew that near-death studies would be a lifelong pursuit. I was, yes, hooked on death.

Suggestions about further directions for my work came from all quarters. Some doctors felt that I should interview as many cardiac resuscitation patients as possible. Since a stopped heart is as close to death as one can get, these doctors felt that the cardiology ward would be an almost endless source of stories.

Those inclined toward anthropology suggested cross-cultural studies: seeking out distant and primitive tribes to see whether they too reported near-death experiences. This was an excellent idea, but one for which I had neither funding nor real motivation. Others suggested asking children whether they had near-death experiences and, if so, determining if they were different from those of adults.

Then came the suggestion that I put symbols on the tops of shelves or the backs of surgical lights and then later ask people who had had an out-of-body experience whether they had seen these symbols, thereby proving a separation of consciousness from the body.

Others—not doctors—suggested that I seek out volunteers who would allow their hearts to be stopped and then restarted in a medical setting. Some even suggested using suffocation. Acquiring near-death experiences in this fashion, they suggested, would allow me to control how long the volunteers actually went without a heartbeat. (On a rather bizarre side note, this suggestion that I stop hearts in volunteers remains popular. The people who present this idea to me usually follow it with an offer to be an experimental subject. I have never taken anyone up on such an offer, and to my knowledge no other researcher has either, although we all have subjects who have suggested such an approach.)

All of these suggestions—focusing on cardiac arrest patients, pursuing cross-cultural studies, rigging lights and shelves with telltale symbols—have been tried over the years by competent researchers, who deliver a variety of results.

But none of these approaches has gone very far in answering the question of what happens when we die. For me, the question is a philosophical one that can only be answered with an adequate theory of logic. That is why I wrote in the first draft of my book that, "for reasons I shall much later explain, I don't think a proof of life after death is presently possible."

Instead of acting on any of these suggestions for further study, I set out on my own path: to devise a form of logic that could reason through the thorny questions of life after death. Devising such a logical framework is a vast project. For one thing, the notion of "life after death" is a self-contradiction. In Aristotelian thought, self-contradictions are not allowed. Rather, the primary basis of Western thought is "the law of the excluded middle": Every statement is either true or false. This means, of course, there is no gray area.

To answer the question of whether there is life after death, one has to overcome the inherent self-contradiction in the notion. Filled with hubris, I set out to do just that: to develop a logic of nonsense.

I soon realized that developing this new logic was—and is—a long-term project. Plato first worked on the problem in the fourth century BC, and since that time hundreds of other philosophers have worked on similar systems of logic. Yet no one has ever resolved the problem of this self-contradictory question: *What happens when we die?* I have tried my best to resolve this problem and am still working on it to this day. If I don't resolve it with the discovery of the new logic I have been seeking all this time, the advancements I have made will be passed on to the next generation of logicians to continue the struggle.

In the meantime, though, I became embroiled in a more immediate problem: the battle between religious people and New Agers over exactly what it was I had discovered in near-death experiences. Both of these groups believed the same thing—that near-death experiences are proof of life after death. And members of each group wanted me to publicly agree with them.

In part I could understand why. The publisher of the mass market paperback version of *Life After Life*, in his zeal to sell books, had added this subtitle to the cover: "Actual Case Histories That Reveal There Is Life After Death." I never, however, implied that in the book. Rather, I declared openly—in both the book and my lectures—that these experiences were *not* proof of an afterlife. I also declared that my work was not scientific.

I wasn't trying to be cantankerous in making such a statement. Rather, I was speaking the truth. If I made a positive statement about the afterlife and later my method was shown to be defective, then those who had taken comfort from that statement would be propelled back into grief *and* they would be angry with me. As a result, I found myself disappointing many people who wanted me to state positively that I had proven the existence of an afterlife.

But I couldn't do that. It would be many years before I could cross the line into such certainty.

CHAPTER TEN

～

W ith the publication of *Life After Life*, two major forces in my life collided: success and illness.

My professors, all of whom were proud of me and glad that I had introduced near-death experiences to the world, treated me with great respect. Over the years since *Life After Life*'s publication, people who don't know the facts have assumed that both the medical school and the medical profession ostracized me for introducing this subject to the collective consciousness. That was not true. The book was such a measured—almost restrained— view of a truly sensational subject that the medical profession saw it for the genuine work of discovery it was. Doctor after doctor has liked the matter-of-fact way in which the book was written, which means I carefully avoided any sensationalism. "Nothing but the facts," one doctor told me. "That is the sign of two things: great material and great scholarship."

Apparently the public agreed with that assessment because the book was selling at a stupendous rate, and dozens of media outlets wanted to talk to me. The problem was that I rarely wanted to talk to them.

My undiagnosed thyroid problem—myxedema—had taken a turn for the worse. The disease first hinted at by my uncle Carter when he felt my cold forehead on a hot day outside a Walgreen's drugstore when I was a teenager had become steadily worse. That strange tingling in my throat had intensified into a presence that prickled and called for my attention almost constantly.

Over the past few years various doctors at student health services had looked down my throat and declared that I had nothing to worry about. Some of them believed that I had only swallowed something hot. An ear, nose, and throat man recommended by my father declared that I was only victim to too much schoolwork.

After hearing these diagnoses, I tried to ignore the feeling of something being in my throat as well as other changes in my body. Despite running several miles per day, I was gaining weight at an alarming rate. I took my files to another doctor who declared that I was working too hard *and* eating too much. Before long I became so heavy that running wasn't possible.

Then I developed patches of blotchy skin on my face and hands. My father noticed immediately and diagnosed it as a skin fungus. He had me go to the drugstore and purchase a tube of tinactin. When that didn't help, I went to a dermatologist who gave me a cursory once-over and declared the bleached-looking patches to be "idiopathic vitiligo," meaning that its cause was unknown.

I was given all of these wrong diagnoses before I started medical school. Now that I was almost finished with medical school my symptoms took an even more sinister turn.

I felt totally out of energy—*dragging* is the word that comes to mind. But when I mentioned my profound fatigue to one of my fellow students, he looked at me with strong disinterest and said, "Medical students are supposed to work themselves sick and tired."

Oddly enough, when he said that we were studying hypothyroidism. I remember reading that patients with this disease are always cold and sleepy. I looked up from the book and said to myself: *That must be terrible, because I'm always cold and I'm always sleepy and I don't have thyroid deficiency.*

I began to lose hair. Once again a doctor said that was normal. Men lose hair as they age, I was told.

I kept going to doctors with myxedema symptoms that were right out of the medical books, and still they were not heeded. One of those symptoms was carpal tunnel syndrome. I went to the rheumatologist with a painful hand affliction and told her about all of my symptoms, from the strange feeling in my throat to the loss of hair. She put her stethoscope on my chest and remarked at how low my heart rate was. She asked, "Were you an athlete, Ray?"

Since I used to run ten miles a day, she discounted my slow heart rate as a sign of fitness rather than a sign of thyroid disease. And she discounted my carpal tunnel syndrome as pressure on my hands from picking up big bags of groceries. The lack of energy? "You're a medical student. You're supposed to be tired."

Every one of my symptoms had an alternative explanation. Yet no one in my profession looked at me as a whole person. Had they done so, they might have diagnosed my thyroid deficiency, which, if left untreated long enough, becomes myxedema madness, a cognitive deficit caused by the lack of thyroid production. At its extreme, myxedema madness mimics schizophrenia with a constellation of psychotic symptoms that includes delusions, visual hallucinations, auditory hallucinations, loose associations, and paranoia.

Through no fault of my own, I was headed down this dangerous road. My symptoms had been ignored by doctors, misdiagnoses had been made, and now I was slowly going mad.

The first real sign I had was a sensory one. I began to feel that I was pushing my way through an atmosphere as thick as mud, a gelatinous mass that was virtually impossible at times to move through. I remember once walking to a podium to deliver a lecture and wondering if I could even speak after the walk up the aisle. I was that tired.

As these feelings intensified I began to feel isolated and depersonalized, as though I were living behind a glass barrier, separated from the world. I'd had those feelings years earlier, but now I was having them in very powerful and meaningful ways. Once while driving in the hills of Georgia, for instance, I felt as though I needed to get out of the car and try to literally shake off this feeling. At other times I would be distant and nonresponsive during important conversations, as though I were watching events on television and didn't have to respond.

Some people thought I had become a snob because I had written a bestseller. That wasn't the case at all. My thyroid level was fluctuating wildly, and I was at the whim of those fluctuations. Sometimes I felt better, sometimes worse, but I was in a gradually diminishing mental state because my overall thyroid level was crashing.

I can't deny that the book's success put the spotlight on me and at times the heat from that light became quite uncomfortable. To tell the truth, success completely freaked me out.

Over and above everything else, what bothered me most were the fundamentalist Christians who began to write hostile letters, some of which contained nothing but raw and unbridled anger. "I believe in Jesus. How about you!" wrote one woman, who then proceeded to tell me that I was "letting the devil out of his box" by exploring near-death experiences.

The main complaint from these fundamentalists was that people of all religious beliefs or even none at all would report seeing beings of light and would often describe those beings as "God." This description was highly offensive to the fundamentalists. They said that seeing God wasn't possible for most people. Only those who were godly—like them—could see God, they declared. What these others were seeing was Satan himself, they reasoned, and therefore near-death experiences were the work of the devil.

That was difficult reasoning for me to wade through. At first I tried to laugh it off, but when I discovered to my dismay that these fundamentalists had little or no sense of humor, I simply tried to ignore them. That proved to be impossible since they were among the first on the line during call-in radio or TV shows.

These fundamentalists made the media interviews even tougher than they should have been. And those interviews were tough enough on the best of nights. In those days media interviews were long and serious affairs—not like today when I am usually on for just three minutes between the story about the trained chimpanzee act gone bad and the release of green turtles in Miami.

In those days I had to get on a plane and fly across the country to an airport where a serious young woman would pick me up and then race me to a studio for a lengthy interview.

Since I wasn't familiar with many of the interviewers, I didn't know if I was going to be in the studio with someone who would carry on a rational conversation with me about mankind's most pressing question or an ignoramus whose main task would be to create a sensation or, worse, just start a fight.

I have to say that most of the interviewers were good to excellent. But there were some utter and complete morons who discredited the rest of their profession. Perhaps the worst was Lou Gordon of Detroit, Michigan. Even after all these years of being exposed to the best and worst of the media, I have never encountered a media person more vile than Gordon. Apparently other guests would agree with my assessment. Gordon took great pride in agitating his guests to such a degree that they would frequently stand up in mid-interview and walk out of the studio. If they took a hike at the beginning of the ninety-minute show, Gordon just sat back and talked about whatever was on his mind. He called himself a "man of conscience, man of truth," so you can imagine the high-handed rhetoric that came out of his mouth.

When I met Gordon, he was all smiles. He greeted me in the station's lobby and shook my hand. Then we went into the studio, and I sat down for what he promised the audience would be a fascinating hour of conversation about a subject of great concern to us all. It was when we started talking that Gordon revealed his fangs. He immediately accused me of fabricating the case studies in *Life After Life*. When I denied doing that, he insisted that I had at least stretched the truth about them. He knew I had stretched the truth, he said, because they all had similar elements!

I tried to explain to him that many if not most human responses have similar elements and that this fact alone made near-death experiences fascinating. He would have none of that. He was trying to make a name for himself by tarnishing mine, and there was nothing I could do about it. No matter what I said he belittled it, declaring that I was a fraud and had made up all of my data! I thought about standing up and leaving but didn't because I felt that to do so would imply that I was lying.

In retrospect, I can see that the subject of near-death experiences punctured his shell of rigidity and somehow represented a threat to his belief system. He was not an open person and could not deal with a discovery that didn't fit into his worldview. Other interviewers occasionally responded this way as well. When they did, this serious area of study I had worked on for years was turned into a circus sideshow. It was disturbing to me at the time because it forced me across the line from being news to being entertainment.

Today, however, it doesn't bother me when I am interviewed by an unpleasant talk show host. I have processed such experiences at a higher level in my mind and now realize that I have to talk to the ill-informed and the ignorant as well as the intellectuals and the curious. But I was young then and had thinner skin. And of course, I was ill.

If one good thing came of my time in Hades with Lou Gordon it was book sales. The next day the regional sales rep called to tell me that my "fabulous" interview with Gordon had pushed sales in Michigan through the roof. He didn't seem to notice that the previous night's interview had been mean-spirited and contentious. His eyes were focused on the numbers, and he liked what he saw.

"Any chance you can get on Lou's show again?" he asked naively.

I was young and taking my success as an author very seriously—too seriously perhaps. The same went for criticism, which at times felt withering when it came from those around me.

One of my greatest critics was a fellow student in graduate school at UVA. He pretended to be a friend, but I began to find out that he was talking about me behind my back. Finally, Dr. George Ritchie, then as now a man whose opinion I respect greatly, took me aside one day and said, "Watch out for this guy. He's green with envy of you."

I didn't know what it was about me that this man envied. He frequently came over in the evening for visits with Louise and me. Initially I spoke freely with him about the near-death experience case studies I was gathering and the nature of the research I planned to do. Soon, however, I had quit talking to him about *anything* I was doing. He had begun to talk about my research to other people at the university, trying to poke holes in it or using half-truths to debase my work. I heard that he was also talking about me and my work in fundamentalist terms, declaring that God would let only the truly religious see a heavenly light and not some of the heathens I was interviewing. Therefore, he said, near-death experiences were the work of the devil. Which meant, of course, I was working for Satan.

In a word, I would call him a "phony." Members of my family, including my wife, didn't view him that way at all. They continued to stay in touch with him and listened quite seriously to his assertions that I was involved in something demonic.

Eventually, when I became totally fed up with this man's toxic nature, I asked him to stay away from my family and asked them to stay away from him. They insisted that I was taking his affronts too seriously, while I felt that they were being too casual with my reputation.

My anger at their continued friendship with this man turned to rage when he wrote and printed a booklet—a sort of anti–*Life After Life*—about the evils of my research. The booklet contained the fundamentalist argument against my work. And worse, it contained personal information about my life that could only have come from members of my family.

They now understood why I wanted them to pluck him out of their lives. But it was too late. I felt betrayed, even by my wife. We had two children, I had a best-selling book, and I was about to become a full-fledged doctor. But our relationship was shot. No matter how we tried, we both knew that our marriage was doomed.

CHAPTER ELEVEN

~

For the next four years I put my medical residency on hold and toured the country giving lectures. It's hard for many people to believe that I could do this, but there were few doctors who wanted to be psychiatrists in those days, and the medical school was willing to accommodate me. Plus, it was a badge of honor for a student from the Medical College of Georgia to be in demand on the lecture circuit.

Even though I was no longer in a medical setting, I was dealing with people all over the country who approached me and told me about their near-death experiences. Hence, I still was dealing with human psychology on a very deep and interesting level.

We had moved back to Virginia by then, and I was frequently called in for consultations with doctors at UVA when a patient had an NDE and the doctors didn't know specifically what to say to the patient about the experience. Talking openly about death and dying was still very difficult for many doctors, especially the older ones who had swept the topic under the rug for so many years.

Of course, that wasn't true of Elisabeth Kübler-Ross. Presenting research on near-death experiences had been relatively painless for me among my colleagues, but it had been almost disastrous at times for Elisabeth. I think the reason lay in her personal style. Elisabeth was not only outspoken but at times confrontational. And she considered herself a medical intuitive who spoke freely of premonitions, often saw and spoke to ghosts (one even wrote her a note after she handed the spirit a pen and paper), and had a spirit friend named Salem who was a seven-foot-tall Native American.

Elisabeth would commonly talk to patients about their pending death. She did not feel comfortable lying to a severely ill cancer patient by telling him or her that a long life still lay ahead, and she did not feel comfortable when other doctors did so. If she heard a doctor tell a dying patient that he or she would be fine, Elisabeth would frequently step in and contradict her colleague right there at the patient's bedside.

She believed in transparency and felt that both patients and doctors would be better off facing the truth. By doing that, she reasoned, dying patients would get the love and care they deserved and not be sloughed off to a room far from the nursing station where they would be treated as though death were a contagious disease.

Elisabeth became interested in death through her compassion. She began to study dying patients and was the first to analyze death so closely that she outlined the five stages of grief and dying: denial ("I feel fine, this can't be happening to me"), anger ("Why me? It's not fair!"), bargaining ("Just let me live to see my children graduate"), depression ("I'm going to die, so what's the point?"), and acceptance ("I can't fight it, so I may as well prepare for it").

Like me, Elisabeth was willing to take the road not traveled. She explored everything she could in the realm of the supernatural. She did this, she said, because she had learned from her work with schizophrenic patients that sometimes they responded better to talk therapy and loving understanding than to drug therapy. Thinking like this has found a place in twenty-first-century medicine, but in the 1960s it put Elisabeth decidedly outside the box.

That was okay with Elisabeth. She liked being outside the box. Her mind wandered freely and took her to unexplored places. I once read one of Elisabeth's journal entries about a trip she and her family took to Monument Valley on the Navajo Reservation in New Mexico. She said the landscape had an "eerie familiarity," as though she had been there before. She let her mind ask questions, "no matter how far-out they seemed," and soon she wrote a journal entry:

> I know very little about the philosophy of reincarnation. I've always tended to associate reincarnation with the way-out people debating their former lives in incense-filled rooms. That's not been my kind of upbringing. I'm at home in laboratories. But I know now there are mysteries of the mind, the psyche, the spirit that cannot be probed by microscopes or chemical reactions. In time I'll know more. In time I'll understand.

Elisabeth's free-exploration of ideas put her—as one of my colleagues so wryly described her—"in a distant orbit." She became involved with a trance channeler near San Diego, California, who had founded the Church of Divinity. The channeler, whom she always called "Jay B.," promised to introduce her to spirit entities that she could talk to and that would respond to her.

The channeling was done in a building called "the dark room," so named because all the windows had been covered to keep out light. There Elisabeth was joined by as many as twenty-five people who sang a soft rhythmic hum in total darkness while Jay B. gathered the psychic energy necessary to channel the entities.

Elisabeth was truly mesmerized by the events of the dark room. During the first weekend she spent there she was introduced to a spirit being named Salem who knew a great deal about her life and became her lifelong friend. She claimed to have even received telephone calls from him.

Elisabeth returned to Chicago, where she was living at the time, and told her husband Manny about the strange events in California. His logical mind could not understand what his curious wife was doing. Then one day Salem called the house and Manny answered. After talking to the channeled spirit for several minutes, Manny had an epiphany about his life. A few days later he asked for a divorce.

Saddened but undeterred, Elisabeth moved to California and lived in a trailer home in Escondido. There she built a healing center where she lived with her spirit guide Salem.

She continued with her death and dying studies there and would frequently lead weeklong workshops for medical students as well as for the terminally ill and their families. Anyone interested in death and dying for any reason was welcome at Elisabeth's seminars.

She continued to attend dark room sessions with Jay B. and firmly believed in his powers as a channeler. Not everyone did, however. Some thought that his channeling was a hoax and that he was not really at the front of the dark room at all when he was channeling but was actually roaming around the room pretending to be the spirits he "channeled."

In the midst of this controversy, Jay B. once told a roomful of people that if they turned on the lights during a channeling session, the spirits would be harmed. Apparently the spirits didn't know this. During this session a female spirit named "Willie" supposedly turned on the lights to expose a totally naked Jay B., standing before them in a deep trance.

The room went into a panic as hands groped to turn off the light. Jay B. continued in his trance as though nothing had happened. It was an eye-opening moment for many of the dark-roomers. After that, rumors started about sexually abusive events taking place in the dark room. The Church of Divinity began to crumble.

Eventually Elisabeth lost trust in Jay B. Her house next to Jay B. and his wife was nearly destroyed in a mysterious fire in 1983. When she ran to Jay B.'s house to get help, he opened the door only slightly and talked to her but offered no help.

That was the breaking point for Elisabeth. She sold her California property and moved with Salem to Virginia to start an AIDS orphanage. (She started this beautiful little institution in the Shenandoahs in the house that my wife and I would sell to her during our divorce.)

I had known Elisabeth Kübler-Ross for several years by then. Shortly before *Life After Life* was published, Egle sent the galley proof to Elisabeth to get a comment. Like me, she had discovered that there is a similarity in the events that take place among people who are dying. She had broken these events down into four distinct phases that a dying person goes through: the sensation of being out-of-body; the feeling of being made of energy or spirit; being guided by a guardian angel; and having the sensation of being in the presence of God. Since *Life After Life* appeared to be competing in the same field, we didn't expect much of a comment from her, if anything at all. To our surprise, however, she wrote a wonderful introduction to the book, from which I quote here:

> I think we have reached an era of transition in our society. We have the courage to open new doors and admit that our present-day scientific tools are inadequate for many of these new investigations. I think this book will open these new doors for people who can have an open mind, and it will give them hope and courage to evaluate new areas of research.
>
> Dr. Moody's findings are true, because they are written by a genuine and honest investigator. *Life After Life* is also corroborated by my own research and by the findings of others.

In addition to writing the introduction, she mentioned that she would be speaking at a community college in Georgia and asked if I could come and meet her, which I did willingly.

I listened to her impassioned and sometimes funny lecture and then went backstage to meet her. At the small champagne party after her talk, she seemed to know who I was even before I introduced myself. She approached from across the room and held out her hand.

"Are you the young man who wrote *Life After Life*?" she asked.

When I assured her I was, she asked, "How did you get all of those wonderful case studies?"

"Well, I just talked to people," I said.

That night we had a somewhat heated discussion about life after death, one that started with her assumption that my research
had proven the survival of bodily death.

"It doesn't," I said to Elisabeth. "It only proves the *appearance*
that we survive after death. The only way to prove we survive is to
communicate with a person who is truly dead."

She looked at me incredulously.

"How can you hear all of these stories and not believe that we
survive death?" She became so agitated that she lit up a cigarette.

I shared my feeling that proof, not belief, was the goal of my
research.

"If you *believe* in life after death, then none of this research is
necessary," I said. "But if you want to *prove* life after death, then
our research has only begun."

"Nonsense," she said. "You have consistent stories of dozens of people who have died and returned, all telling of similar
events. It's like the early explorers who returned after finding a
new country. When enough people came back with the same stories, there was no more denial about whether the country existed.
You don't have to see something firsthand to know it exists."

Elisabeth couldn't understand why I wouldn't say that I had
proven life after death. Since I'd had the same experience she'd
had with dying patients, she thought I would certainly take the
same leap of faith she had. In fact, my attitude puzzled her so
much—vexed her, really—that we decided to never talk about life
after death again.

From that point on our relationship was based on humor.
I used to make up stories about her as she sat at the table and
laughed. One was about one of her chickens dying and how she
gathered the chicks around to explain to them that their mother

was traveling up a dark tunnel and meeting a large "chicken of light." Elisabeth would sit there and laugh and laugh as I poked fun at her. When I hear people say that they found Elisabeth to be dour, I always think of those times when I made up stories for her and made her laugh.

Elisabeth wanted me to go on the road with her and proclaim a belief in life after death. I appeared with her many times, but always disappointed her by stopping well short of declaring that I had discovered proof positive of life after death. I would go so far as to state that the near-death experience is a sort of entrance way to what awaits us after death, but I would also point out that just because one has seen the pearly gates doesn't mean there is permanent residence inside.

"But at least we've made it to the pearly gates," I would tell the audience. "Perhaps soon we'll be able to take a peek beyond."

Elisabeth wasn't the only person disappointed by my lack of a stance on the afterlife. Many people in the audience would be stunned to learn that I didn't think I had found proof of life after death. Invariably one of the first questions when the lecture was over would be: "Did I misunderstand you? You *do* believe in life after death, correct?"

The truth was that I was a skeptic in the ancient Greek sense of that word ("one who goes on inquiring"). A skeptic in that fascinating ancient culture was not someone who was a naysayer—as we think of skeptics today—but rather a seeker who had decided not to reach a conclusion.

A skeptical frame of mind is the best one to have in the world of research. Think about it. If everyone else is rushing to draw a conclusion but you are not rushing in the same direction, you are likely to see side-paths of inquiry that nobody else is seeing because they are busy running with the herd.

Indeed, skepticism in the ancient Greek sense of the word is mind-expanding because a skeptic in that sense is trying *not* to reach a conclusion. As the popular definition of a skeptic has changed over the years to refer to a naysayer, a skeptic has become someone who denies the existence of anything that he or she hasn't personally experienced. A real skeptic is also someone who believes that the only rational means of proving truth is through the scientific method.

Since truth is a moving target, I believe that the only legitimate means of finding the truth is to keep searching for it. As Donald Duck said when he was pretending to be a fortune-teller: "I will gaze into my crystal ball and the future will pass into the past." Or looking at this idea another way—the future is always changing, and the truth changes with it.

My focus has never been on finding what is true. Rather, my focus is one of constant inquiry. As the medieval alchemist Paracelsus said, "A man who wants to write a book first creates a heaven in his mind from which the work he desires flows." I have avoided making that heaven in my mind and stuck with the hard facts instead, a stance that doesn't seem very popular. Most people prefer living in the hard and fast world of what they consider to be "true or false."

I understand, but I can't take them there.

I delivered lectures almost exclusively for four years and then returned to complete my residency. There is a vast difference between medical school and residency. Where med school requires a great deal mentally, medical residency requires raw physical stamina. It is to medicine what boot camp is to the military.

My first rotation as a resident was in geriatrics at the State Mental Hospital in Virginia. I loved working in geriatrics. Being raised as much by my grandparents as by my mother made me feel right at home among an elderly population.

All of the elderly patients committed to this institution were in an advanced state of dementia. There was one man, an insurance agent from Charlottesville, who had occupational delirium, a condition in which he returned to his behavior during all those years as an agent. Every day he would pretend to dress up in a suit and go to work—which was a dinner tray he placed in front of his chair in the recreation room. He would spend hours making pretend telephone calls before going out to make personal visits, which generally had him knocking on the doors of other patients. Sometimes he would stop me and ask, "Excuse me, sir, can you tell me which of these rooms is my office?"

Another patient had been a cleanup man in a barbershop for forty years. He would pretend to sweep around chairs all day. Another man, a former aircraft mechanic, paced the floor with crumpled papers in his hand and shouted orders to phantom employees, demanding that they "get the engines back on airplane number seven!"

Sometimes new patients knew me from having read my book. Some were wary of me because of my notoriety, thinking they had been assigned to this ward because the staff thought they were going to die. In their lucid moments, after I had convinced them that I was just there for medical training and not as a hospice doctor, we had some wonderful conversations.

There was much about the unique and intriguing world of the mental patient that I had forgotten during my four years on the road. I was truly fascinated by the various permutations of the human mind, how age or other factors can change personality and perception and lead normal people to become extreme enough that they no longer fit comfortably into society. Others were just as fascinated as I was. One night I was sitting in the staff room reading when a nurse came in. She sat down to read, but we ended up talking instead about some of the patients on the floor.

"Is it difficult for you to work in a mental hospital?" I asked.

"Heavens, no," she declared. "It's the best place I've ever worked."

"Why?"

"Because," she said in a half-whisper, "it's like working in an art gallery where the paintings are alive and tell stories!"

Not all wards at the mental hospital were as pleasant as the geriatric ward. The maximum-security unit for the criminally insane was a darker and scarier version of the human art gallery that so pleased the nurse and me. The Binion Building, as the ward was called, had about 120 patients at any one time, all of them violence-prone people who had committed an extreme crime that classified them as a violent psychotic.

The law enforcement community was very pleased that I was a doctor at the hospital. My brother Randy was a respected member of the sheriff's department, and they felt that I would be more understanding than most doctors of the demands placed on law enforcement by the criminally minded.

They also appreciated the fact that I didn't use "doctor talk" in discussing these dangerous criminals but spoke to them in plain English, as I did with my brother. And I never made concrete statements about how I thought these patients would behave in a future situation, as other doctors did. On more than one occasion I was backed against a wall and even nearly choked by one of these unpredictable psychotics, and I didn't want a law enforcement officer hurt because I had made an unsafe assumption about a patient's criminal behavior.

I can tell you for certain that the Secret Service never made assumptions about criminal behavior. One night I showed up for work and there were three new files on the desk. When I opened them, I found bright orange cards stapled to the charts emblazoned with the seal of the Secret Service. Written below each seal, in bold black letters, was this admonition:

> If this individual escapes from your institution,
> *do not fail to contact the United States Secret Service!*

In the recreation room I discovered three new patients, all of whom had been rounded up by the Secret Service and dropped at our institution for safekeeping. President Ronald Reagan was in town, and the people assigned to protect him came in advance and institutionalized those who were thought to pose a threat during his visit.

The three men were clearly angry at being arrested and said little over the course of the twenty-four hours they were in our care. But that afternoon, when President Reagan made his speech in Macon, Georgia, all three gathered around the television and watched, silently seething as "The Great Communicator" spoke to a gathering of local businessmen.

Working in a mental hospital was perfect for a doctor like me who wanted to learn about all aspects of the human mind. To this day I can re-create scenes in my mind of patients wandering blissfully around the geriatric ward, talking to people who weren't there or creating scenarios that didn't exist. What world did they live in? What was that world like? I ask these questions to this day.

My time off was spent finding people who had had near-death experiences and talking to them. As a totally passive activity, collecting case studies in near-death experiences was an ideal pursuit for someone with severe yet undiagnosed myxedema. All I had to do was take my $25 tape recorder and a healthy supply of tapes and go by Greyhound Bus to small southern towns where I sat with people as they told their stories. It was another setting, as the nurse had described, like an art gallery where the paintings talked. Only now I was out of the mental hospital and interacting with a population of normal people who had been blessed by a paranormal event.

I never thought of myself as a particularly energetic person. Yet looking back, I see that I must have been. After all, by the age of thirty-two I had acquired two doctoral degrees, taught philosophy for three years, written one of the all-time bestselling books, and created a new field of medical study—*all while I was still in medical school.* Then I delivered lectures for four years, sometimes day after day, telling what I knew about this field I called "near-death studies."

Doing all of this required a tremendous amount of energy. I must have had some secret reserves. Or perhaps it was just my natural curiosity that drove me to greater and greater heights.

But now it was 1985, and things were definitely changing. For the previous three years I had not read a single book. I felt as though vitality and energy had totally left my body, taking my powers of reason with them. I had allowed a money manager to take over my finances, and before long we discovered that he was skimming a large part of my income into his own pocket. Since my wife Louise had suggested him through a friend, I held her responsible. In reality, it wasn't her fault. I had been too passive in the decision to use him, allowing it to be made *for* me instead of *with* me.

I became paranoid and depressed, side effects of myxedema. My marriage was not doing well, and my illness prevented me from engaging very well as a father with my two sons, Avery and Samuel.

In a moment of demented clarity, I saw what my life had become and I decided to wipe the slate clean. I told Louise our marriage was over. We divorced in 1986, and I moved out.

Things didn't get better. I met a woman and we married, but that didn't work. I became both "too distant" and "too dependent" for this independent young psychology student. I tried not to take the rejection personally. I knew she was right, but I was having a serious problem and didn't know what it was. All I knew was that I felt a deep sense of dread, as though nearly every part of my body was telling me in its own way that I was dying. Strangely enough, that seemed okay with me. I had been studying near-death experiences for at least a decade and from all of my interviews had come to feel that the supernatural warmth of a bright and mystical light was likely to accompany my own death. I began to long for that experience. I was ready to die.

I left my job at the maximum-security mental hospital in Milledgeville, Georgia, and accepted a job at West Georgia State College in Carrollton. It was a life-changer for me. My spirits rose as I found myself back in the classroom with students. I found a roomful of students to be a much more positive environment than a hospital ward filled with the dangerously mentally ill, a place where one always had to be on guard for sudden violence from the people being treated. The problem afflicting me, the disease of myxedema that I didn't know I had, seemed to abate. Had it really been a symptom of overwork, as several doctors had indicated? Life seemed better. I felt as though I was going to live.

CHAPTER TWELVE

~

It was now more than a decade after the publication of *Life After Life*, and the field of near-death studies had blossomed, with literally dozens of medical studies having been conducted by a variety of researchers.

I was proud of the field of medical study I had launched and the researchers who had taken my interest in the near-death experience to new heights. These early researchers had bravely decided to go where no investigators before them had gone.

Some of them, like Michael Sabom, MD, and Kenneth Ring, PhD, did very methodical explorations in order to derive hard medical facts. Sabom, a cardiologist in Georgia, examined the claims of thirty-two patients that they had left their body and watched as doctors performed resuscitation in the emergency room to restart their heart. He compared their descriptions of the resuscitation procedures with the educated guesses of a control group—twenty-five medically savvy patients—about what happens when a doctor tries to restart a heart. Sabom wanted to compare the accounts of those who had had an out-of-body experience to the knowledge of the medically savvy patients.

He found that most of the patients in the control group—twenty-three out of the twenty-five people—made mistakes in describing the resuscitation procedures. On the other hand, none of the NDE patients made mistakes in describing what went on in their own resuscitation.

This work was groundbreaking for two reasons: it indicated that people truly do leave their body after a near-death experience, and it also showed that these patients are in a state of hyperobservance in which they can not only see what is going on but remember it too.

Ring, a psychology professor in Connecticut, was hooked on the study of near-death experiences from the very first time he heard a patient's description of her experience of almost dying. In 1977 this woman had experienced a very rapid loss of blood pressure while delivering her child. She reported that the room turned black, and when she "regained consciousness" she was up in the corner of the delivery room looking down on the doctors as they worked to revive her and deliver the child.

She didn't travel up a tunnel or see a being of light, but she did hear a spirit speak to her, saying, "You've had a taste of this. Now you must go back." The voice also told her that the child would be born with heart trouble that would be corrected in time. That all proved to be true.

The woman's story fascinated Ring. The study he devised examined the stories of 102 near-death experiencers and showed that religion is no more a factor in a person having an NDE than age or race. In short, he proved that near-death experiences are equal opportunity events.

In a way, Dr. Melvin Morse, a pediatrician in Seattle, Washington, did the same thing. After treating a near-drowning victim as a resident physician in Idaho, he was drawn to studying the near-death experiences of children. The young girl, whose name was Crystal, was resuscitated after being found at the bottom of a YMCA swimming pool. Although profoundly comatose for three days and thought to be brain-dead, Crystal made a full recovery.

A few days later Morse asked Crystal what happened in the swimming pool.

"Do you mean when I sat on the Heavenly Father's lap?" she asked.

It was not what he meant at all. Morse wanted to know if she'd had a seizure or perhaps was knocked unconscious by hitting the side of the pool during a dive. Still, he didn't correct her.

"That's exactly what I mean," he said encouragingly.

What he heard was an amazing story of angels, a heavenly realm, and an out-of-body experience that allowed her not only to see what was going on at the hospital but to make several visits to her home, her descriptions of which were highly visual.

"You'll see, Dr. Morse," said Crystal. "Heaven is fun."

The look of sheer confidence in Crystal's eyes led Morse to start a decades-long search for the uses and meanings of near-death experiences. In his first book, *Closer to the Light,* he hit on a youthful version of Ken Ring's conclusions with his finding that children are just as likely to have near-death experiences as adults; their experiences differ in only one primary and logical way, he discovered: children don't have very extensive life reviews. After publishing his book, Morse went on to research the long-term transformative effects of the near-death experience. In his book *Transformed by the Light,* he concludes that people who have near-death experiences—especially those that include a vivid experience of light—are blessed with a post-traumatic "bliss" syndrome that results in a positive personality transformation.

Many other researchers were examining such topics as the link between NDEs and the great philosophical truths, or NDEs that take place as the result of combat. I was proud of the work I had spawned by writing *Life After Life* and read carefully the research published in medical journals. I also became very good friends with many of the researchers, so much so that they often wanted me to join them as a research associate. I was honored to be asked, but I always said no. I felt that proof of life after life would come from a breakthrough in logic, not from scientific studies.

As I told my colleagues, "You guys have taken my work into the mainstream. Now I have to wade out a little farther."

As had happened in the past, I stepped into that deep water unexpectedly. And there I found myself in a world I never thought I would explore—the world of past lives.

I was lecturing in Florida on near-death experiences when a woman in the audience asked whether I believed in the existence of past lives.

I shrugged. When I lecture, I always get a large number of questions about other extra-normal phenomena that have little or nothing to do with near-death experiences. Most of them involve UFO abductions, spoon bending, psychic healing, and, yes, past-life regressions.

For some reason these questions irritated me at that time. I had no real explanation for any past-life events, nor did I have any real interest in researching them. I was like William James, who, when asked about the Hindu belief in the rebirth of our spirits into other beings, just shrugged and said that his cultural upbringing didn't make the discussion of that subject a live option for him.

That is what I said that night in Florida to the poor woman who asked me about past lives. I told her I just wasn't interested in the subject. "It's not a live option for me either," I said. And anyway, "everyone who gets regressed says they were Cleopatra or Napoleon. How many can there be?"

The crowd laughed, and the woman was probably humiliated. I felt comfortable in my ignorance.

That comfort lasted for approximately twenty-four hours. I went to visit Diana Denholm, a psychologist who used hypnosis in her practice. Denholm had originally used hypnosis to help people stop smoking, lose weight, even find lost objects. Then some strange things started happening. Patients under hypnosis would start talking about events from past lives, usually when she had regressed the patient to recover a lost or traumatic memory. Known as age regression therapy, this technique was designed to find the source of phobias or neuroses that are creating problems by taking a person back through his or her life layer by layer, like an archaeologist digging through layers of time. Sometimes, however, the technique would take patients beyond the layer of their birth date and they would talk about a long-ago era as though they were right there in the here and now.

These trips through time frightened Denholm at first. She thought she had done something wrong in her hypnotherapy or perhaps had uncovered multiple personalities in her patients. But as these events continued to happen frequently, Denholm discovered how to use them to treat her patients.

After she began to use past-life regression therapy with patients, she found it to be very effective in treating their disorders. "Maybe you should try it instead of condemning it," she said to me. Feeling appropriately chastised, I decided to do just that.

That very afternoon Denholm offered to do a regression. She seated me in an overstuffed recliner and led me, slowly and skillfully, into a deep hypnotic trance. She told me later that I had been under for about an hour. And yes, during that hour I was aware of being Raymond Moody and being under the guidance of a hypnotherapist. But at the same time I found myself going back through nine lives, each in its own distinct incarnation and civilization. None of these lives were like a dream; rather, they were like reality, and visiting them was like watching a movie. The colors were real, and the events unfolded from their own inner logic and not from any manipulation or wishing on my part. I know I was not trying to determine the plot because I could have done better than what happened.

Of the nine lives, only two took place during time periods I could recognize, and both of those were set in ancient Rome. I was unable to date any of the others except to say that they were in prehistoric societies or had no historic context at all. That isn't to say that they didn't all seem familiar. Each dripped with nostalgia for me, so much so that I thought I was remembering actual experiences.

Here, in chronological order, is the series of lives I lived through past-life regression.

1. Proto-Human

In my first life I was a prehistoric version of a man, a proto-human with no ability to speak. I lived with a group of other beings in nestlike structures high in trees. We had helped one another construct these homes. We lived in groups because we knew there was safety in numbers. I also knew that we valued beauty and had carefully selected the trees we lived in to take advantage of the pink flowers that carpeted the tops of the trees.

I knew we were manlike, although we moved in a bent-over fashion with our center of gravity in our hips. We were fruit-eaters, and I remember eating a fruit that was red and full of seeds, like a pomegranate. Eating it was so completely real that I could feel the juice run down my chin and hear the crunch of the seeds as I chewed.

We stayed high in the trees, but I had what felt like a fatal attraction to life on the ground. At one point an animal with the appearance of a wild boar ran beneath the tree, and we all began to jump around emotionally. Since we were unable to speak, we could only let our emotions speak for us.

During my regression I had no control over when I passed through each lifetime. As a result, I soon left my life in the trees and went on to another life.

2. Primitive Africa?

In this life I was about twelve years old and living in a tropical forest with a group of people. I guess it was in Africa, but that is only a guess.

When this hypnotic adventure began, I was in the woods looking down a slope to a stark white strip of beach on the shore of a calm lake. That was where the houses of my village were located.

The houses were platform houses set about two feet off the ground on stout poles that had been pounded into the ground.

The walls were made of woven straw. Each house had four walls and contained a large single room in which each family lived.

At one point I was a little boy fishing on the shores of the lake. The men were out on the lake in rough wooden canoes. I wanted to be with them, but I was too young, so I just cast my net from the shallows and caught a small amount of fish.

I jumped forward to a later time in this life and found myself climbing up a rugged blue-and-black mountain with a group of warriors. We were carrying long spears and wooden shields that were brightly painted with images of animals. Each of us was brightly decorated with war paint. I had the feeling we were going into battle because we held our breathing to a minimum during the climb to keep from making too much noise.

I was tired and frightened during the climb and had a deep desire to return to the familiarity and safety of the village by the lake. Then this life faded to the next.

3. Death by Drowning

In the next episode I was an old and muscular man with long silver hair and blue eyes.

I was building a boat in a large room that was long and entirely open to a river on one side. In the middle of the room, running the length of the building, was a nearly completed boat. On the wall behind me hung primitive boatbuilding tools.

With me was my three-year-old granddaughter. She watched timidly as I demonstrated the various tools of my craft. I could see her peeking over the tops of the gunwales as I pounded caulking into the boat's joints to make it waterproof.

I launched the boat into the river and then picked up my granddaughter for the first voyage. We were enjoying the boat's maiden voyage, but pleasure turned to terror when a wall of water came up the river and capsized us.

I was thrown one way and my granddaughter the other. I thrashed in the water, trying to reach her, but she was gone in an instant, sucked under by the wave's powerful undertow. When I saw her disappear beneath the waves, I gave up. I remember going underwater and forcing myself to stay down because I was filled with guilt that she had died on my watch.

In my hypnotic state, the fear was vivid. My heart pounded and my blood pressure rose as I heard the water rushing around my ears. The water gagged me as I went under, and my guilt intensified as I realized all of the life she would miss due to this one poorly-timed journey.

The guilt changed to ecstasy as I neared death. At that point a bright light engulfed me and I was overcome with total bliss. I knew at that point that everything would be all right for my granddaughter and myself.

I went to the next life.

4. The Mammoth Hunter

I was suddenly plunged into a band of people hunting woolly mammoth.

As you can imagine, it is not my style to take on something so big. But in my hypnotic state, I could see that we were not well fed and were truly desperate for food.

We wore animal skins that covered our chests and shoulders and were barely adequate for the frigid climate. Our legs were bare, and our private parts were not adequately covered at all. The primitive clothing wasn't our only concern. The weapons we used were stones and tree branches.

We had trapped the mammoth in a gully and were trying desperately to beat it to death. The mammoth would not give up easily. He grabbed one of the tribe members and with a clean, efficient move crushed his head. We were horrified at the violent loss of our tribal member.

As the fight continued I seemed to leave my body and drift above the scene. Then I went on to my next life.

5. A Worker Among Workers

I found myself in the midst of an enormous public works project. I was not the king in this scenario, nor was I even a foreman. I was simply a worker among workers. I had the sense that we were building a road system or perhaps an aqueduct, but I couldn't tell for sure.

My wife and I lived in one of the apartments that were lined in a row along the road. It had only one room and was dominated by a sleeping platform that we both lay on as soon as my workday was complete.

We were starving to death. All of the workers were, most likely from a famine. My wife lay on the platform looking very gaunt. I had the idea that she was waiting for her life to just completely flicker out.

I had a great sense of guilt because my wife was dying and I could do nothing to protect her. I think all of the workers were in a similar situation. They were tired from the moment they got up in the morning. I remember struggling up a hill to get to our work site and then looking grimly at the day's task.

Behind me, my wife was dying and there was nothing I could do about it.

6. Lion Food

I faded into the next life and was finally somewhere I recognized, ancient Rome. Once again I was neither emperor nor nobleman, but lion food. I was in a pit and about to be devoured as public amusement.

I had long reddish hair and a mustache. I was thin and wore a leather loin garment. I knew something of my background. I was from the area now known as Germany and had been captured by the Romans during a military campaign.

I had been used to carry booty back to Rome and was now about to be put to death for the amusement of the Roman populace. I could feel the energy of the desperately hungry lion that was caged next to me in the pit. I looked up to the crowd for mercy but felt a sickening tightness in my stomach as I realized there was no mercy.

I saw a man in the crowd with long brown hair that was closely cropped on the top of his head. His left eye was pink and infected, creating a sinister look on his emotionless face. He stared at me and put a snack in his mouth, chewing as he chuckled. My death was clearly nothing more than an amusement for him.

There was a blur of activity as the lion sprang from the cage and knocked me to the floor of the pit. The last thing I remember was being pinned against the dirt as the lion made for my skull.

Mercifully this life faded into the next.

7. Noble Death

I was in a beautiful apartment that glowed with the fading light of early evening and the yellow light of several oil lamps that gave the marble walls of the room a glistening luster.

I was wearing a white toga and lying on a sofa shaped like a modern-day chaise lounge. I think I was in my forties and had the physical softness of a bureaucrat unused to hard labor. I remember a feeling of complete complacency, to the point of sleepiness, as I lay there looking at my son, a dark-haired fifteen-year-old who was becoming increasingly frightened by the scene beneath our balcony.

"Father, why are those people trying to get in here?" he asked.

In my complacency, I felt as though this had happened before and was nothing to be concerned about.

"Why, son," I said, "that's why we have the soldiers."

"But, father, there are so many of them," he said. The fear in his eyes caused me to get up to see what he was talking about. I walked to the balcony and saw a handful of soldiers pushing back a huge mob that was about to become too surly to handle.

At that point I knew there was good reason to be frightened. I looked at my son, and I could tell from his response that he was alarmed at the look on my face. That was the end of that lifetime, but I have a feeling it ended shortly thereafter at the hands of an angry mob.

8. Murder in the Desert

My next life took me to a mountainous area in the deserts of the Middle East. I could tell that I was a jewelry merchant who lived up in the hills behind my small but prosperous store.

I spent the day appraising gold and silver and precious stones. I also traded with the caravans that passed by on a trade route.

I made a lot of money and spent it on my home, which was my pride. It was a wonderful reddish-brick place with a porch situated in such a way that the evening breeze swept in and cooled the entire house. The view from the porch was spectacular and took in the entire valley.

The house was spacious inside, with a forest of pillars that held up the roof and made the interior look very grand. I could remember happily whiling away the time with my wife and three children.

One day after work I returned to a strangely quiet home. I felt a sense of doom as I walked in because quiet was not common around the house. As I went into the bedroom I found my wife and three young children dead, brutally murdered and left in pools of blood.

From the feeling I had while under hypnosis, I could tell that I would never recover from this tragedy. I don't know when I died, but I could certainly tell that my life was over from that day forward.

Thankfully, I moved on.

9. *The Chinese Artist*

In my final life I found myself to be a Chinese artist. A female Chinese artist.

I moved quickly through childhood and adolescence and could see several scenes in which I was painting. Sometimes I saw my work from the perspective of the canvas and could see my brush strokes laying down dabs of paint.

I had several detailed yet fragmentary memories from this life. At one point I was talking to a friend in the middle of a street when a brilliant light suddenly flashed over us. We were puzzled, so we went to a local wise man and told him what we had seen. He was puzzled too, but told us that we were not the only ones to report such a flash to him. Still, he didn't know what we had seen.

At another point in this life I went to a large stone house to visit an elderly aunt. She seemed to be in her sixties and was beaming at my arrival because I was her favorite niece. Her gray hair was pulled back in a braid, and she was standing on the porch in cotton pants and a shirt.

The next scene I remembered was the last day of my life. I lived in impoverished conditions, in a small house with only a bed, a stove, and an area where I could set up my painting equipment. This was not a safe area of town. On this particular night a young man came into the house and strangled me. Taking none of my earthly possessions, he took just the one thing that had no value to him—my life.

As I died I rose above my body. I felt concern for the young killer who stood above my body, clearly proud of his work. I wanted to know what had made him so unhappy that he wanted to kill an old woman. Although I tried to communicate with him in my out-of-body state, I couldn't reach him. Instead, I just faded away.

In a few moments I left these past lives where I had found them and returned to full consciousness. Denholm was sitting next to me, coaxing me out of my hypnotic stupor and back into the current world. "Current world" was a phrase I had never before thought of, but it came to mind now. Before this session I would have assumed that this is the "real world" and those others a dream. But now, lying on a therapist's couch, I realized that "current world" described quite well the place I had returned to. I now almost believed I had lived before.

CHAPTER THIRTEEN

~

A mazing, isn't it?" asked Denholm when I came out of the hypnotic trance.

I nodded my agreement, but didn't say anything. What I had experienced seemed genuine and had nothing to do with wish fulfillment, as I had previously believed. After all, when had I ever wished to fight a wooly mammoth or dreamed of being a financially destitute female artist in China?

I was somewhat embarrassed by what had just taken place. I no longer felt the same about past-life regressions, and Denholm seemed to recognize that. She laughed at me as I pondered what had just happened. I mumbled a few words of doubt, but then admitted with conviction that I had truly ventured into my distant past.

"It depends upon your point of view," she said. "I have my point of view. What is yours, really?"

I didn't know. These experiences were not like dreams. At the very least, they represented a unique level of consciousness, one with its own distinct features. They had a feeling of familiarity to them, like remembering last summer's trip to France. They were distinctly memory, not made-up events.

Still, they were somewhat different from memory. While in the regression state I was able to see myself from various perspectives. For instance, when I was in the lion pit I watched part of the action through my own eyes and then from a perspective above, where I could actually see myself in the pit being stalked by the lion. The same was true when I was the boatbuilder and the Chinese artist.

Part of the experience happened as if seen through my own eyes, and part as though I were outside my body, watching myself from a third-person perspective.

I tried to gather my thoughts. I didn't want to jump to conclusions about these experiences. The brain has more depth and creativity than most people give it credit for. It is also a sort of a magnet for memory, collecting bits of random information that stick for seemingly no reason.

Yet these experiences were different. They were so vivid that they seemed to be proof of reincarnation. Or at least possible proof. To tell you the truth, I didn't know at the time what these nine lives were or meant. I just knew that I was being guided down a path I had never been down before.

I spent an hour or so in the fading light of the Florida afternoon writing down everything I could remember about the nine lives I had just experienced through Denholm's hypnotherapy.

When that task was completed, I did what I had done with near-death experiences: I wrote down questions that would help me think about this new mystery that had come into my life.

- How can these strange journeys be explained? Especially to those who don't believe in reincarnation? After all, atheists have near-death experiences yet still don't believe in God. How does, say, a staunch Baptist explain a vivid past life experienced during hypnotic regression? Are these merely what happens when the mind creates entertainment at the unconscious level? Jung thought the unconscious mind is far more active than most believe. Are these voyages to a past life merely self-created television programs?

- Can medical conditions, both mental and physical, be affected by past-life therapy? I was especially interested in the effect this therapy might have on phobias and anxiety disorders. Regression therapy was often effective in treating these problems. Can past-life therapy reveal even more that could relieve these and other medical problems?

- How can we explain truly mysterious cases?

I had heard about mysterious cases of past lives but had largely ignored them because, as I said before, they were not a live option for me. After this session with Denholm, I became at least a partial believer. I wanted to hear some of the more undeniable cases.

I decided to break down past-life regression into its various traits, just as I had done in defining and naming near-death experiences. It was the eleven common traits of near-death experiences I delineated that gave therapists, doctors, and patients themselves the information necessary to understand these puzzling events. I was surprised to discover that the same kind of work hadn't yet been done with the phenomenon of past-life regressions.

As I had done before with near-death experiences, I decided to start researching this field with my students. As I've already mentioned, I was teaching psychology at West Georgia State College in Carrollton. Although it is a conservative college in the midst of the Bible Belt (Newt Gingrich taught history there!), the Psychology Department could have come right out of Berkeley. Rather than focusing on mainstream psychology, which involved behaviorism, cognitive therapy, and other types of therapy that can be empirically proven, West Georgia had branched out into paranormal phenomena. When William Roll, director of the Psychical Research Foundation, joined the department in the eighties, he introduced courses on ghosts, near-death experiences, hypnosis (which is now mainstream), and modern-day shamanic psychotherapy.

When I mentioned at a staff meeting that I was going to dissect the phenomenon known as past-life regression, the other professors were delighted.

When I told the students my plan, they were overwhelmingly delighted at the prospect of being used as pioneering guinea pigs in such a study of successful past-life regression therapy. They knew this could be breakthrough work in understanding reincarnation and its possible therapeutic uses.

I culled my classes and found fifty students who were open to new experience and had flexible hours. Then, not wanting to limit myself to a student population, I put out the word that I needed experimental subjects from the general population.

Overall I formally studied about one hundred subjects.

First I did group regressions. Taking about twenty subjects at a time, I performed group hypnosis with them. Thanks to George

Ritchie, I knew how to perform hypnosis. A hypnotist himself since the age of twelve, Ritchie enrolled me in a class at the International Association of Clinical Hypnosis *after* privately teaching the arts of hypnosis to me himself. The protocol was to hypnotize the group to see if the results were better than those from individual regressions. The lives recalled in these group sessions weren't as complete or colorful as those recalled in the individual regressions; most likely, I assumed, because it was more difficult to relax in a group. That result was totally expected.

But in the course of doing these group regressions I discovered an extrasensory phenomenon that truly puzzled me: on several occasions, subjects on one side of the room would experience virtually the same past life as a person on the other side. This happened frequently. For example, when a woman described herself as a ballet dancer wearing blue tights and dancing in front of a large audience on a brightly lit stage, another woman on the other side of the room was describing almost the same experience. In one session a young man described a crime in which he had been involved in nineteenth-century New York City that led another person in class to gasp. As it turned out, the notebook he was about to read from describing his own regression contained the story of a nearly identical crime, his too in old New York.

These seemingly psychic connections added another piece to the puzzle but did not help make its form comprehensible. They just made the puzzle bigger.

The second phase of the studies focused on individual regressions, which involved hypnotizing the individual alone in my office. This usually made it easier on my subjects because they didn't feel the group pressure, nor did they have a fear of revealing their emotions in public. I would have subjects lie on my office couch and then leisurely work them into a deep hypnotic trance.

Individual sessions rarely failed and were very revelatory.

For example, a woman I'll call Anne had been afflicted with both high blood pressure and panic attacks for several years. She took hypertension medication and watched her diet carefully, but still experienced high blood pressure and severe anxiety.

Anne volunteered for the regression study because she knew that I was interested in finding out if ailments could be treated successfully with this kind of therapy.

Once I got her hypnotized, Anne found herself in a small city in Egypt. She came into this life on what was surely its last day. The city as she described it was surrounded by hordes of an unnamed aggressor. Most of the army defending this town had been killed in battle, and now panic was in the air as the invading force moved in for the kill.

After the session, she described what she had seen:

"It finally became horrifying. I could see people running all around me through the streets as attacking soldiers chased us, slashing and stabbing with their weapons.

"The soldiers were very selective in who they killed first. They would hit the women with their fists to get them out of the way but keep them alive. It was the men they wanted to kill first.

"They would stab them several times, pouring their blood all over the streets. Then they would trample over their bodies and search for other men. Soon it was clear that only the women would be left.

"I was a young woman in these scenes, and I felt a very intense pressure to get away. Yet it was no use. Every way I looked was blocked. I found myself running with other women, but there was really no place to run. We just pounded aimlessly through the streets. Everywhere I turned there seemed to be another group of foreign soldiers.

"Finally they closed in on the women. One by one we were pulled out of this huddled group by soldiers. I was one of the first to be taken. An angry soldier pulled me toward him, and when I resisted he simply drove a knife into my stomach and let me fall."

That was the last thing Anne remembered.

As Anne described the events in her mind, she was breathing heavily and perspiring. She seemed to choke with fear. Although the fear had been intense and the experience was "clearly more than a dream," Anne was greatly relieved by the release of emotions that it provided. It would prove to be a catharsis for the anxiety in her life.

Over the next few weeks, Anne opened up and confronted her fears. She talked freely with her boss, who caused her much anxiety because he never seemed happy with her work. She also began to talk to her husband about her concerns over their lack of intimacy.

As she opened up, her blood pressure dropped into a more normal range and her anxiety attacks all but disappeared.

How did she interpret the events of her past-life regression? She didn't believe that it truly happened. Instead, she felt that it was an experience generated by her mind that was symbolic of the out-of-control feelings she had about life. And what happened to those feelings? "All other experiences pale in comparison to the fear I felt when I was chased and killed by invaders," she told me. The past-life regression served to calm her down while giving her the courage to talk with others about issues that had caused that "pressure cooker" feeling inside of her.

The physical or mental status of many of the subjects in my studies improved as a result of their regressions. And many had theories about why their illness improved or why it had occurred to begin with. A number of them, to my great surprise, took a metaphysical view of their illness. They believed that we might choose our illness just to know what the experience of that illness is like.

Other subjects saw their regression as the ultimate mind-body connection. They believed that a past life can afflict the body with a pathological condition. Once that past life is confronted through regression therapy, the disease is likely to abate.

In fact, one study showed some promise using this method. Johannes Cladder of the Netherlands treated twenty-five patients with difficult phobias (defined as patients who had already received psychotherapy and in some cases been hospitalized). Of those twenty-five patients, twenty eliminated their phobias through past-life regression therapy.

Many in my study didn't feel that they had plunged backward into a past life, but had very intense experiences nonetheless. And then there were many who had no doubt at all that they had gone back in time. Some of these subjects even felt as though they had proven the existence of past lives.

One such person who was not in my study was the late Ian Stevenson, a colleague of mine at the University of Virginia. He examined several cases suggestive of reincarnation, mostly in India, where it is easier to talk about past lives because of the large number of Hindus, who believe in reincarnation. Stevenson's research was painstakingly detailed: he checked people's stories with detective work that sometimes took him all over the country and into many living rooms.

Typical of his work was the story of Parmod Sharma, born in 1944 to the family of a professor living in Uttar Pradesh, India. As Stevenson wrote:

> When he [Sharma] was about two and a half, he began to tell his mother not to cook because he had a wife in Moradabad who could cook. Later, between the ages of three and four, he began to refer to a large soda and biscuit shop which he said he had in Moradabad. He asked to go to Moradabad. He said he was one of the "Mohan Brothers." He claimed to be well-to-do and to have had another shop in Saharanpur. He showed an extraordinary interest in his biscuits and shops. . . . He related how in the previous life he had become ill after eating too much curd and said he had "died in a bathtub."

Stevenson interviewed the child in India. Then he talked to the family and learned that they had no previous knowledge of or friendship with anyone named "Mohan." Stevenson then found that there was a biscuit shop in Moradabad known as the Mohan Brothers. He found that they owned another biscuit shop in Saharanpur. He also discovered the existence of a brother who had died of a gastrointestinal illness. "Did he die in a bathtub?" asked Stevenson.

> The witness of the Mehra family stated that Parmanand tried a series of naturopathic bath treatments when he had appendicitis. He had some of these treatments during the days just before his death but did not actually die in a bathtub. In a letter dated September 7, 1949, Sri B. L. Sharma stated that Parmod had said he died of being "wet with

water" and that he [Sri B. L. Sharma] had learned (presumably from the Mehra family) that Parmanand had been given a bath immediately before his death.

And so on. Stevenson researched dozens of reincarnation cases around the world, taking what another researcher called "the direct approach to the issue" by researching these stories with as much care as possible. Although his research remained largely anecdotal, it did not rely on the word of the person having the experience. He checked and rechecked and left us with a large body of meticulous work on the subject.

And then I found some stories that seemed to almost research themselves.

One such case was a health professional in California who told me that he was regressed and found himself as a French nobleman who lived on an estate in the South. His wife's name was Sylvie, and they had two children. He was among the most powerful men in a large region. From a chateau he directed hundreds of peasants.

"The most specific scene in the regression was one in which I was riding horses with my wife through well-manicured woods up to the chateau," he recalled. "She had on a bright red dress made of velvet and was riding sidesaddle."

Not only was this man able to recall his name, he also had a date from the 1600s fixed in his head. With date and name in hand, he searched the birth records preserved over the centuries and located that record of this nobleman's birth, as entered by a parish priest.

This gentleman had no recollection of ever having seen or heard this name before remembering it during regression. Nor was there any reason that this wealthy farmer in 1600s France would have appeared in European history books. This man felt that this experience was proof that he had lived before.

Although this man's story would not be adequate proof of reincarnation for the scientific community, it was part of a growing body of past-life stories that certainly went a long way toward changing my mind.

I came to look at these regressions in many ways. Sometimes I thought of past-life experiences as a means of escape from a boring day-to-day existence; at other times I found them to be a fascinating means devised by the brain to avoid mental pain by reframing an issue as something that took place in a past life. Other past-life experiences seemed to be a form of ego inflation or a means of explaining or avoiding depression. And then some past-life stories made me outright believe in reincarnation and our ability to remember past lives.

One statistic in all the research I read stood out for me. It came from a study done by Dr. Helen Wambach, who found that 90 percent of all people who attempt hypnotic regression are able to recall events from a past life. I asked myself: *How can a person's "past life" seem as real as their current one? If these are just "flights of fancy," as some claim, why then don't they seem like fantasy? And why does solid historical information pop up in the middle of these experiences, confirming that they may be real?*

In the end I couldn't answer any of these questions, and no one who ever researched this subject has been able to either. Although these stories are interesting, they are just that, stories. There is no empirical way to study past-life regressions. And even though much of what people say they have witnessed during their regressions can be proven to be historically accurate, there is no way for researchers to tell how much of the information in the regression was captured by the unconscious mind through television or books or other sources. That leaves past-life regression studies as simply a collection of interesting and very puzzling stories that can be neither proven nor denied.

CHAPTER FOURTEEN

E ven though I was unable to determine the reality of reincarnation, I still examined all of the successful past-life
regressions in my study as well as many others from regression therapists. I found what I came looking for to begin with:
identifiable traits that are present in regression experiences.

Traits in an experience like this are important. They tell researchers, clinicians, and experiencers alike what can be expected during regression, whether one believes they are truly
reincarnation experiences or not.

I am not saying that a regression experience that doesn't have
all of the dozen traits outlined here is not really a regression experience. I am saying, however, that anyone undergoing a successful past-life regression therapy can expect several of these
symptoms to arise.

Trait 1: Past-Life Experiences
Are Usually Visual

Most of my subjects have said that their past-life experiences consist largely of sensory images. These images are usually visual, but a few subjects have also described odors and sounds. The subjects say that the images are more vivid or "real" than those in ordinary daydreams and usually do not seem distorted in the bizarre ways familiar to us from the dreams we normally have.

The past-life images are usually described as being in color. Here is one such example from a woman who was regressed and found herself as a farm boy in the late 1800s.

> I was an eighteen-year-old boy, sitting on the back of a wagon with my feet dangling down. I was right there. I could see my feet hanging down off the back of the wagon as clearly as if I had done it only five minutes ago.
>
> In the same life, I was out working on a fence and I could see a snake at my feet just as plain as if it were right here in front of us. I ran to get away from it and fell and hit my forehead on a rock. The pain was so vivid that I had a headache when I came out of the trance. I also thought that blood was dripping down my face even after I came out of hypnosis because I could still feel it from the rock that caused me to bleed in my trance.

This is just one example of the way the senses are stimulated by past-life regressions.

Less often, a past-life experience takes place in the form of thoughts. However, a lack of sensory images doesn't make a past-life experience any less compelling. Regressions that consist only of thoughts can be as moving and captivating as those composed of vivid and vibrant imagery.

Trait 2: Past-Life Regressions Seem to Have a Life of Their Own

The scenes and events that take place during a past-life experience seem to unfold of their own accord, as though their outcome and progression are somehow independent of the conscious control of the person undergoing the experience. As a result, subjects usually feel as if they are witnessing events, not making them up, as a daydreamer would. Subjects frequently describe the feeling that they are watching a movie that seems somewhat familiar.

A good example is my own regression. When I found myself as the Chinese lady artist, I was not sitting there making decisions about what would happen next. I had the feeling that I was just sitting there watching a movie. The events unfolded scene by scene. For me it was just like watching the big screen. Everything was in vivid color and detail. All I had to do was sit there and watch.

Trait 3: The Imagery Has an Uncanny Feeling of Familiarity

The past-life experience is often permeated with a sense of familiarity, even nostalgia. The feelings that subjects describe are very similar to the common experience of déjà vu, the feeling that you have already done or seen whatever you are currently experiencing.

These feelings of familiarity may range in intensity from a vague sense of remembrance to a sudden and forcefully recaptured memory of long-forgotten events.

One such example is the regression of a patient I'll call Neal. This Georgian, who was raised Southern Baptist, went to the unlikely lifetime of a monk in Ireland. He had many experiences that were steeped in familiarity, but perhaps the most vivid was watching with another monk from the top of a hill as some elderly farmers were murdered by thieves.

It was horrifying, but very much like I had seen it before. We had just topped the hill and were looking down at this farm when we noticed a band of horsemen riding toward the farmhouse. The old farmer and his wife came out to see who was coming and these horsemen rode right up to them and hit them with swords and clubs. We then watched as they dismounted and began ransacking the house.

When I saw this in my trance, it didn't surprise me. I had this feeling of "Oh yeah, I remember that." It was horrible, but I had been there before.

Sometimes the experience awakens a feeling of homesickness for the apparent previous life. The subject may even come away drenched with nostalgia for the lost world.

One of my patients went back to ancient China in his regression and was able to visit with his mentor, an old sage who had taught him well throughout the years of this previous life. Now he likes to come in for regressions just so he can visit with that old man!

Trait 4: The Subject Identifies
with One Character

People undergoing a past-life regression identify themselves as one of the individuals in the unfolding drama and maintain this uncanny sense of being that person despite what may be profound differences in physical appearance, life circumstances, occupation, sex, or a host of other factors.

For example, one of the students in my college class reported with all apparent sincerity and conviction that he was a merchant living in Turkey hundreds of years ago.

In another regression, a young southern housewife described her sense of having been an African warrior in the dim primeval past.

> I suddenly found myself as a black warrior dressed in nothing but some kind of grass skirt to cover my privates! My jet black skin was covered with very elaborate patterns of war paint that zigzagged all over my body and made me look extremely fierce.
>
> I now realize the purpose of the war paint. It may seem silly to us now, but when I was in my regression I found myself looking into the eyes of this man coming up against me in warfare. He had war paint on, and the paint helped strike terror in my heart! The purpose of the paint was to add to the emotional impact of hand-to-hand combat.

This identity may linger even into the post-hypnotic period. The subject may come away feeling quite sure that he or she actually was that person in a past life. *And* they might have been.

Trait 5: Past-Life Emotions May Be (Re)Experienced During a Regression

Subjects usually report that they feel the emotions of their character in the regression. Thus, in one of my own regressions I actually felt some (mercifully not all) of the terrible terror as a lion leaped on me in the closing moments of my life in a Roman coliseum.

This emotional "reliving" is also quite apparent to the hypnotist conducting the regression. The subject may scowl with anger upon "reliving" an event in the regression that has made the subject furious. Tears may flow copiously as a subject, seemingly "back in time," experiences a particularly touching or sad episode. The entire gamut of human feelings from tender love to fury may come to the surface during a deep past-life regression.

The emotions may be so powerful that it is sometimes helpful for the hypnotist to reassure the subject that he or she has "lived through" the experience in a lifetime long ago and there is no reason to fear or be distressed by the situation anymore.

Trait 6: Past-Life Events May Be Viewed in Two Distinct Perspectives: First and Third Person

Those undergoing a past-life regression may have a bilocality of perspective that enables them to (re)view the events from either a first- or third-person perspective. In the latter perspective, sub-

jects become a "disembodied" observer of the action from outside the body of the person with whom they identify.

For example, a young student of mine described a scene from
her regression in which she believed she was a coachman in early
nineteenth-century Europe. At one point in the drama she saw
the action from the point of view of the coachman himself. She
seemed to be in his body, viewing the road in front of him from
his perch on top of the coach. She saw the horses racing forward
and even felt the wind. Then there was an accident, and the coach
overturned. Suddenly she found herself viewing the scene from
above, looking at the coachman's twisted body in the wreckage
below.

Another example comes from a snippet of a patient's regression.

I saw a man walking along the road in a blousy outfit like
the ones they wore in the Renaissance. I found that I could
watch the action from above this man as well as from his
perspective. I could switch perspectives at will, almost like
a TV station can switch cameras to change points of view.

Trait 7: The Experience
Often Mirrors Current Issues
in the Subject's Life

In most of the past-life regressions I have conducted, the events
and situations that unfold reflect the dilemmas and conflicts
faced by the subject in his or her present life. Usually, these connections are obvious.

For example, one of my patients was involved in a stressful relationship with a somewhat older woman who was attempting to dominate him. As a result, he was feeling helpless.

When he was hypnotized, a past life unfolded in which he had been a slave girl in an ancient Middle Eastern city.

I remember being in a very beautiful palace in a place that seemed to be rows of apartments where slaves were coming in and out, taking care of these beautiful women. I was one of them, the kept flock. We were kept as concubines for someone, a sultan perhaps.

On the one hand, it was great there because we were completely comfortable with all of our material needs taken care of. On the other hand, it was the worst sort of hell because we had no inner freedom.

This regression was intriguing to me because in it he was a subjugated woman. *Why?* I wondered. After further therapy sessions, I was able to conclude that, to him, all women are in a state of subjugation. And since his current girlfriend had subjugated him, he was feeling like a woman.

The relationship of his past-life experience to his present life's circumstance then became quite clear.

But while such connections may be plain to an observer, they might not be so clear to the subject. This comes as no surprise to me. We humans routinely blind ourselves to even our most pervasive hang-ups by relegating them to our unconscious minds.

Some subjects don't need to have the similarities between these past lives and their current one pointed out. Many people awaken from the hypnotic trance with the full insight that the past-life experience they just had was very similar to problems in their present life.

This tendency for past-life memories to echo current circumstances sometimes leads people to wonder whether their present difficulties result from unresolved problems in a past life.

That the regression experience resonates so closely with one's current issues is part of the rationale for past-life therapy, which gives therapists a window into those issues.

Trait 8: Regression May Be Followed by Genuine Improvement in Mental State

Catharsis is a psychological process in which pent-up feelings are allowed to be expressed, resulting in an enormous feeling of release and relief. This process often permits people to arrive at a new perspective on a sticky conflict or to make a needed change in a stressful or debilitating relationship.

Catharsis of this kind often occurs during a past-life regression, as in the case of a young man who was locked in bitter resentment toward his younger brother. During his past-life regression, this young man, who saw his brother as taking all the resources and attention of his parents, witnessed a previous life in which he had lived in a jungle, apparently in South America, as an old man who was a member of a native tribe.

In that life, there was an elderly woman whom the subject identified as his present-life brother. The elderly woman didn't look like his present brother. He made the connection through intuition that the person in the regression was his brother.

In this regression scenario, the old man (the patient) was deformed and relied entirely upon the old woman (his current brother) to take care of him. She had, in essence, sacrificed herself for him.

The subject emerged from the past-life regression with a new feeling of love for his brother. He now felt the balance was being restored. In a past life his brother had graciously borne the burden of caring for him. Now it was his turn to care for his brother.

As a result of this past-life regression, the subject told his younger brother of his feelings, and their relationship reached a new and more satisfying equilibrium.

All of my patients have reached some point in their regression that intersects with one of the problems that plague their life. It might not be very dramatic in some cases, but they all say, "Since that regression I understand more about. . . ."

Trait 9: Regressions May Affect Medical Conditions

In rare instances, subjects may report dramatic improvement in physical symptoms following a past-life regression, and sometimes even spontaneous resolution of those symptoms. For instance, a woman I'll call Lisa had frequent and severe headaches. Although she had no organic problems, like a tumor, and she had long ago stopped drinking anything containing caffeine or alcohol, she was unable to control these insidious headaches without a large daily dose of aspirin.

She came to me for a hypnotic regression, "just to see what is there." I took her into a hypnotic trance, and there she experienced very bad times in an ancient city made of stone. Here is what she had to say after the regression.

I was living in this city as it was being attacked by invaders from another country. In the hypnotic trance I could see them descending upon the city, ready to rape and pillage.

> We were all terrified. I could see people running all around me as the attacking soldiers chased us, slashing and stabbing with their weapons.
>
> I could see myself. I was a young woman dressed in white clothing. I was trying very hard to get away, but there was little reason to try, since the soldiers were everywhere.
>
> Suddenly I was caught by several of the invaders. One of them held my arms and one of the others hit me on the head with a club. The pain was incredible. They hit me several times and then dropped me. I could feel my brain swelling as I slowly died.

The pain was apparently overwhelming. As she lay on the couch with her eyes closed, hurt was evident in her face and voice.

Discussing this terrible death proved to be a cathartic experience for Anne. She experienced a great deal of emotional release while describing the emotions of the past-life moment. As we talked about her hypnotic regression it became clear that there were many sources of stress and panic in Anne's life. By using this powerful regressing experience, we were able to pry into many of the emotions she had kept pent up. Subsequently she was able to take less pain medication for her headaches.

The occasional cases like Anne's are evidence of the powerful connections between mind and body.

Trait 10: Regressions Develop According to Meanings, Not a Historical Timeline

If a subject were to be regressed to a dozen distinct "past lives" over the course of a year, a series of lives that center on an emotional or relationship theme would most likely emerge, not a series of lives appearing in the chronological sequence in which they would have been lived.

For example, a male subject might have a couple of experiences that deal with his attitudes toward women, followed by a series of two or three lives that embody various ways of dealing with aggression, followed by a cluster of lives in which issues of dependence on others seem paramount.

The primary feature revealed in the "past lives" of a subject seems not to be that person's role in history but rather his or her psychological and spiritual development. This is yet another feature of these experiences that can make past-life therapy successful.

Trait 11: Past-Life Regressions Become Easier with Repetition

Generally speaking, the more a person tries, the easier it becomes to enter into a past-life experience.

That proficiency seems to come with repetition. The subject also feels more and more natural and at home with the regressed state.

There may be temporary setbacks—resistance to the hypnotic state may reemerge owing to present-life stresses or other distracting factors—but overall the subject will enter the regression state more and more easily.

Trait 12: Most Past
Lives Are Mundane

Although popular belief has it that almost everyone who has regressed to a past life claims to have been Napoleon or Cleopatra, I
have found only a few subjects who identify with a known historical figure. Instead, most of the lives that appear are typical lives
of the periods to which the subjects regress.

This isn't to say that people willing to undergo hypnotic regression wouldn't like to be Joan of Arc or General Ulysses S.
Grant in their past life. However, they are usually disappointed
to find themselves in a past life as an ordinary French citizen or
just a foot soldier in the Civil War.

In my book *Coming Back: A Psychiatrist Explores Past-Life Journeys*,
in which these traits were originally published, I expressed a lot
of doubt about past lives. I am still doubtful. Even after experiencing nine convincing lives of my own during one extraordinary regression session, I don't know to this day whether I
believe they truly represented reincarnation. "Traits are like
tire tracks on a dirt road," a professor once told me. "They might
let you know that a vehicle has been there, but they don't nec-
essarily tell you what kind of vehicle it was." Still, I have soft-
ened my viewpoint on reincarnation substantially. As I wrote
in *Coming Back*:

> As a result of my research, I knew I was no longer a skeptic,
> but I didn't know what I was no longer skeptical about. Isolat-
> ing the traits or "symptoms" of PLRs meant that I knew what

to expect from a hypnotically regressed patient. But it didn't mean that what they were perceiving had really happened.

The mind likes to please and for that reason it is highly suggestible. When given the opportunity, it will fill in gaps with great aplomb. And when given the focused leisure time that hypnotism presents, it will often occupy itself with self-made fantasies. . . .

. . . Skepticism aside, past-life regression analysis clearly offers some important new opportunities for the psychotherapist. After conducting almost one hundred hypnotic regressions for my research, it was obvious to me that this method offers a quick and innovative way to find out, at least partially, what is troubling the subject.

In almost every hypnotic regression that I had conducted, the subject's "past life" memory mirrors a conflict in his or her current life. By hypnotically regressing them, I am able to arrive at the root of the problem quickly. Instead of spending hours of couch time, the patient is able to fully face his problem early in therapy and spend more time learning to cope with it than finding it.

Believers in reincarnation say that this mirroring occurs because a conflict in a past life must repeat itself life after life until it is resolved. Maybe this is true. Who's to say otherwise? But I do believe that past-life regressions deal with mental conflict in a unique and effective way, one whose value should be realized even by those who don't believe in past lives and reincarnation.

That is why I continue to examine them.

CHAPTER FIFTEEN

*

What happened next in my life was both the worst and best that could have happened at that time.

Let's start with the best, then go to the worst, and finally return to the best for what I would consider to be a happy—although nearly deadly—ending.

My co-author Paul Perry had been working with me on the past-life regression studies, and we were writing a book. Our agent, Nat Sobel, had sold the idea of doing this book to publishers in several countries, and now we were fully funded and writing to a deadline of the summer of 1990.

I was relieved to have a large book advance. Despite my professor's salary and speaking fees as a frequent lecturer, I was in financial straits. Not only was I paying for my boys' schooling, but I had also made a terrible financial decision in hiring a business manager who was taking as much as 50 percent of my income.

If you ask how I could do such a thing, I can only shrug and blame it on my myxedema. As my thyroid levels had dropped over the previous couple of years, I found myself making more and more critical errors in judgment. There are many examples, but by far the worst were the ones I made that led to the heavy hit to my income. By the time I was able to break the contract with this business manager, I was deep in the hole.

Writing this book was my way out. Not only had we received a fairly substantial advance from the American publisher, but they also had high hopes for it becoming a bestseller. If that happened, my financial woes would be over.

I was thrilled to be working on a book that would sum up my regression studies. As with near-death experiences, I had stumbled onto a field of study that had not been fully explored. I had dissected near-death experiences, taking them apart like no one had before me. Doing that let me focus my life on a single worthwhile project. So it was with my past-life regression work. I saw the use of past-life regressions as an innovative form of psychotherapy and felt that this book would be a substantial addition to the arsenal of tools available in the field of psychology. I was proud of my efforts.

By August 1990 the book, which we titled *Coming Back: A Psychiatrist Explores Past-Life Journeys*, was completed. The manuscript landed on the publisher's desk on August 2, 1990—the day Iraqi leader Saddam Hussein attacked Kuwait.

About a week later the editor called and was bubbling.

"This book's remarkable," she said. "I think we've got a bestseller here."

I was thrilled. All the way through the process I had received accolades. The editor's assistant had read it and called with a story about her own past-life experience. The copy editor had

gone through it and written me a long letter that included stories from friends who'd had very successful past-life regression
therapy. And more than a month before the book's publication
date, I received a call from a very effusive marketing director. He
too believed that the book was destined for the top of the heap.
There was plenty in my book for both sides of the argument, he
declared. Believers and nonbelievers alike would be able to see
the value in what I'd done.

Then my editor added, "If Saddam Hussein doesn't get in the
way, you'll have a hit on your hands."

Saddam Hussein! I had been watching the gathering storm in
Iraq on television, but now I began to watch it in a more personal
way. As the weeks progressed I saw in my mind two lines con-
verging on one another, one representing the coming war and the
other the publication of my book. When I expressed my concerns,
both the editor and marketing director told me not to worry. The
company had a big press tour planned for *Coming Back*, and there
was no way to back out of it now.

"These press tours get a life of their own," said my editor. "If
we stop it now, we'll lose our momentum."

Always a fan of the news, I now watched it obsessively as U.S.
forces took up positions in Saudi Arabia and waited as President
George H. W. Bush and Saddam sparred verbally on the international stage.

"We have you booked on TV and radio in more than twenty
markets," said a marketing assistant. A slight hesitation in her
voice made me feel uncomfortable.

It was now the first week in January, and I was feeling the
stress of the situation. Press tours are stressful anyway, but this
one was worse. I would have to fight major world events for a few
moments of airtime on TV or radio. And then, who cared? The

hint of World War III would trump anyone's interest in a book on past lives. I knew it would certainly trump mine.

And then there was that tingling in my throat. I was feeling weak and cold, and the constant tingling was foreshadowing worse to come.

I begged one more time to delay the press tour. Bombing was going on in Iraq and had been for weeks. And President Bush was promising war if Saddam didn't withdraw from Kuwait by January 15. Couldn't they postpone this tour for a month or two?

I made that appeal on January 13, three days before I was to go on *The Today Show*. When bombs started falling on the fifteenth, I was sitting in a hotel room getting mentally prepared for my appearance the next day. The marketing assistant called with disturbing news. The appearance had been canceled until a later date.

And so it went in the next twenty or so markets. I would get on an airplane and fly to a city where a chirpy public relations escort picked me up at the airport and drove to a television or radio station where a distressed producer would meet us in the lobby with the bad news that our talk show or TV segment had been canceled. The explanation, of course, was that all of the airtime was being devoted to the war in Iraq.

Some of the stations taped interviews with me that they saved for later. I don't know if these interviews were ever broadcast or if the producers just felt sorry for me. In fact, after traveling to about ten markets, I didn't care much about anything. The tingling in my throat, which had become very noticeable in the days leading up to the tour, had worsened substantially since the tour began. Now it had become a presence, an almost electrical feeling I could not ignore.

By the time I got to California I had done only one live interview and taped maybe three. The stress of the situation caused me to get sick faster than I had ever experienced before. I had to wear a thick sweater underneath my blue blazer, and in San Francisco I stopped at a men's store to purchase a pair of ski gloves.

When I went into the studios with my escort, the producers looked at me nervously. The escort looked at me with the same discomfort, and when I caught sight of myself in windows on the street, I was alarmed as well. My eyes looked dead, and my face had the pallor of someone who was near death. I didn't care. In fact, I wanted to die.

I called my co-author, Paul Perry, and told him I wanted to die. I was sitting in a San Diego hotel room, and all I could think about was climbing out the window and letting gravity take its toll. I was cold, tired beyond belief, confused, and losing the color in my vision.

Paul talked me down, but I still couldn't get it out of my head that suicide was the only way out.

By morning things were better. I boarded the airplane for Atlanta and fell into a fitful sleep. But once I woke up again and tried to weave through the airport, I could feel my energy slipping and with it my mental stability.

Back in Carrollton, I was surrounded by sympathetic friends who, knowing what this book meant to me, dropped by one by one to see how I was doing. Some clearly thought I was drunk when they spoke to me because I was slurring my words and not making much sense. The ones who knew I didn't drink insisted I see a doctor as soon as possible. I made an appointment to see my doctor on Monday, but by Sunday I had gone completely mad.

With a large bottle of the painkiller Darvon in my possession, I got in my car and drove to my office at the college. There, I reasoned, I would lock the door and take a dose of painkillers sufficient to kill me.

In my office I opened the bottle of Darvon and poured the pills out onto my desk. Then I began to take them several at a time with gulps from a can of Coca-Cola. I took about two dozen of the pills and then sat down at the desk. For some reason I called Paul Perry.

"I've done it," I said with a note of finality.

"Done what?" he asked.

"I've taken pills and I'm dying," I said. "I want you to be the last person I talk to."

I could hear the controlled panic in Paul's voice as he started to ask a series of questions: "What did you take? How many did you take? Where are you?"

I became somewhat angry at the line of questioning. I could tell that he wanted to get enough information to somehow intervene from Arizona. But I didn't want an intervention. What I wanted was good conversation in the final moments of my life.

"Look, Paul, I have researched death, and I know it's nothing to be afraid of. I will be better off dead."

And that was genuinely how I felt. Myxedema madness had put me in the throes of a paranoia and despair so great that I felt everyone would be better off if I was no longer around. No amount of talk could convince me otherwise. Paul suggested a number of possible solutions to my problems, including an agent and CPA to straighten out my money problems and a new press tour to arouse interest in the book. I would hear none of it. I was ready to die.

"You know, Paul, being alive holds more fear for me than being dead. I have talked to hundreds of people who have crossed into death, and they all tell me that it's great over there," I said. "Every day I wake up afraid of the day. I don't want that anymore."

"What about your children?" Paul asked.

"They'll all understand," I said resolutely. "They know I'm not happy here. They'll be sad, but they'll understand. It's time for me to leave."

I could hear someone jiggling the office door knob as we spoke. Then there was a pounding on the heavy wooden door, a couple of raps at first and then a persistent drumbeat. Then a loud voice. "Campus police, open the door."

I ignored the demand and kept talking to Paul, taking a few more pills as we spoke. Within seconds a key was slipped into the door lock and the door sprang open. Policemen rushed in and before I could say much of anything they had put my hands behind me and sat me on the floor.

One of the policemen picked up the phone and began talking to Paul. Apparently Paul asked about the presence of pills, because the policeman began to count the pills on the desk. When he did that, he dropped the phone on the desk and from his police radio he dialed 911.

An overdose of Darvon has little effect on a person until it reaches a critical blood level. Then the painkiller overwhelms the heart's beating mechanism and quickly stops it cold. A dentist friend who had seen someone overdose on Darvon said it was like falling off a table: the person was operating fine until he just dropped to the floor. I knew that the same thing would happen to me shortly. All I had to do was wait. I sat patiently on the floor as EMTs charged up the stairs with their gurney and equipment.

"Are you okay?" asked one of the EMTs.

"Sure," I said, and I was. Never better actually. I was not afraid of death, but I had obviously become very afraid of life.

Things began to happen fast after that. My chest felt very heavy, and I had the feeling of slipping into a dark blue place.

They hoisted me onto the gurney and strapped me in and rolled me quickly down the passageway to the waiting ambulance.

As they loaded me into the ambulance the world around me began to fade. The concerned EMT was in my face, trying to keep me awake. Another EMT was drawing something into a very large syringe, probably adrenaline to inject into my heart. "Better get going," shouted one of the policemen as he slammed the rear doors. I could feel the ambulance accelerate, hitting speed bumps hard as we headed for the hospital. An elephant was sitting on my chest. My eyes were closed, or at least I think they were. Either way, I could see nothing.

My heart stopped.

What happened next is almost indescribable, but I will do my best to make it less so. I could feel myself separate from the world around me. In a funny way it was almost like cellophane being pulled off a smooth surface, one reality separating from another.

I sensed spirits around me, helpful presences, who were there to guide me through this separation. I tried to see these spirit guides, but I could not make them out because I was surrounded by a light that was not of this world. I could hear them speaking, and although I couldn't make out what was being said, their presence was soothing and calm and I felt a radiant love from them.

I didn't have an opportunity to examine myself in this state to see what I looked like or was made of. And I didn't have the time I would have liked to try to make contact with the spirits either. Instead, I felt myself "start up" again as the doctors pumped my stomach and gave me a shot of a stimulant to the heart. The light went away, the spirits were there no more, and I came to in an emergency room.

That's what it's all about! I said to myself as I lay there on the bed. I didn't feel I'd been dead long enough to have a classic near-death experience, but at least I got close enough to see the city limits. I was oddly pleased. After defining, naming, and studying near-death experiences, I could now say I'd had one and, yes, it was real.

I lay in the bed reliving the experience. There was nothing unreal about it. If anything, it was almost mundane, as though I had opened a door and walked into a strange room. I wondered what would have happened if my heart had been stopped longer. Would the spirit beings around me have become visible? And were they people I knew and loved? Would the light have changed and become that palpable and mystical light so many talk about? Would my life have come back to me in a review? Would I have been introduced into a life after life?

I puzzled over these questions for some time and then settled on what I knew—that an extraordinary transformation of consciousness had taken place at the point of death. I did not go into a blackness, as so many assume will happen. Rather, I found myself in a richer, deeper, and more real state of consciousness. I had gone somewhere that so many have described as heaven.

The next day I was transferred to a short-stay psychiatric facility. I expected nothing, really. For most of my life I had gone through periods of being extremely cold, having no energy, and developing the skin disease vitiligo. I had also been extremely depressed, even suicidal.

Yet even with these symptoms in plain sight, no doctor had ever diagnosed a treatable disease. So on this day in February 1992, I expected no meaningful diagnosis from the doctor who had been assigned my case. Still, I spoke politely to him about my medical history and suicide attempt. I noticed that he nodded and took a few notes, as all doctors do. He scanned what he had read and then made a proclamation.

"Oh, Dr. Moody, I'm sorry that no one has ever picked this up. But you have thyroid disease, myxedema," he said.

I was very reluctant to believe that for all of those years I had been victim to such an easily diagnosable disease. He ordered a blood test, and in a few days he came in with the results. I remember looking at the lab value and seeing the number 119. An indication of the amount of thyroid in my bloodstream, 119 was such a low thyroid count that there was some concern among the medical staff as to whether I would get my mental faculties back.

"I think you will," said the diagnosing doctor. "The greatest predictor for recovering your mental abilities is having a high IQ, which in your case means you'll probably make a full recovery."

A full recovery to what? I wondered. I'd had myxedema for so long that I didn't know where a full recovery would take me.

The doctor started me on a course of thyroid medication (slowly at first) that took my blood levels back up to near normal. Soon I was functioning well again, but I was given a big warning by the doctor that at times I have not heeded (as you will soon see): Thyroid levels fluctuate dramatically, he said, and so will your emotions if you don't watch your levels at all time.

My life changed after that. I now knew the cause of my mood swings and the reason I sometimes wanted to kill myself. Like a person with diabetes whose insulin can sometimes swing wildly, I had finally learned that my thyroid could drop in a minute and take me with it. And it has continued to do that, sometimes with horrifying results.

And yes, I still become suicidal at times. I still get into those moods where I wish I was dead, and I can even start to ideate on how I will kill myself. But now that I know the source of these feelings, I am armed with the wherewithal to stop myself and test my thyroid levels.

I have found one positive side to my suicide attempt. Now, when people come to me with suicidal thoughts, I can talk to them with firsthand knowledge about this horrible urge. I freely share my own story of attempted suicide and tell them why I am glad I didn't succeed. I also bring in the data about people who have tried to commit suicide and had near-death experiences before being revived. These people say that they will never again try to kill themselves, not because they fear going to hell, but because they have learned that life does have a purpose.

Still, as a psychiatrist and a human being, I am aware that some people are having suicidal ideation all the time. To address this I give patients that old psychiatric cliché: If you ask one hundred people if they have ever considered suicide, ninety will say they have, and the other ten are lying.

It's funny, but it's true. And it's good to know we are not alone in even our darkest moments.

CHAPTER SIXTEEN

~

For many years I had been interested in reproducing certain aspects of the near-death experience in people who were not near death. For example, being able to re-create a vivid life review *without dying* would be extremely valuable in a therapeutic setting for a patient trying to relive childhood trauma. Another aspect of the near-death experience that would be valuable to re-create would be the ability to see dead relatives. This would be helpful in a number of therapeutic situations but mainly in grief therapy for those with a desire to see the deceased just "one more time" in order to tie up loose ends and make sure the deceased is comfortable in the afterlife.

Over the years researchers have presented a variety of ways to duplicate the near-death experience. Some in the medical profession have even done so without knowing what they were doing. In the 1950s, for example, a German physician named

E. J. Medune developed carbon dioxide therapy: Patients who breathed a gas mixture rich in carbon dioxide reported having reactions very similar to NDEs, including the sensation of zooming through a tunnel and achieving varying levels of cosmic wisdom.

Medune developed this therapy as a means to cure stuttering. It appeared to work well in that regard and even worked as a therapy for stomach ulcers. Subjects in the stuttering and ulcer studies may have achieved some level of transformation (as NDEers do) as a result of carbon dioxide therapy, but that is only my assumption, since the transformative effects of the "Medune Mix," as it was called, were never duplicated.

For me, the most interesting part of the NDE is seeing departed loved ones. Of the nine stages of the NDE, this one seemed the most valuable to grief therapy, the work I was closely involved in.

The most common desire of people grieving over a loved one is to see the deceased again. When the death was very painful, the living person may want to see the loved one again to see if the pain is gone. Other times the grieving person may have unresolved issues with the deceased and wants to resolve those issues face to face. I have had patients who were molested by their fathers and now want to get the pain of the abuse behind them by talking about it with the late perpetrator. Still others are just lonely and need to fill that emptiness with one more loving encounter.

The desire to see a deceased relative was a powerful motivation for many of my grief patients. And for me, not being able to accomplish that goal for them was a great frustration. The ability to facilitate an apparition, if you will, was beyond the grasp of medical science.

Then one day the answer landed on me, literally.

I was browsing the dusty shelves of a used-book store in a small Georgia town. Spying an old book in the psychology section that looked interesting, I reached to pull it down from a high shelf and the book next to it slid out and fell at my feet. I picked up the book and looked at its title: *Crystal Gazing.* My only exposure to such things was in comics: Donald Duck would dress like a fortune-teller to bilk his naive nephews of their allowance.

Ordinarily, I would have put the book back on the shelf and been done with it. But on this particular day I had time to let my mind roam, and I decided to do so with this fascinating tome by a scholar named Northcote Thomas. The introduction by Andrew Lang, an eminent psychologist from the early twentieth century, expressed his belief that the rational medical and scientific community would be appalled by anyone who tried to conduct medical studies on any form of crystal gazing.

But Thomas's work had changed his mind. Now, declared Lang, medical doctors should find research into crystal gazing as being "no more offensive, really, than the dreams of the day or night. They are phenomena of human nature, exercises of human faculty, and, as such, invite study. To shirk examination is less than courageous." The book was dated 1900, and to my knowledge no one in the medical community had taken the Lang challenge and attempted any research on crystal gazing.

As I read on, though, first in the bookstore and then at home, I became fascinated with the possibilities of crystal gazing. I began to study the ways in which other cultures created altered states of consciousness by gazing into crystals, mirrors, or other clear depths, which in general is known as *scrying.* Then I began to research the ancient Greeks, my favorite culture, and the cave warrens they created known as *psychomanteums*, where people would spend weeks in order to connect for just a few moments with the spirits of their deceased loved ones.

As I studied the work of Thomas and other historical accounts of the art of scrying, I began to wonder if I could take it out of the realm of art and turn it into a science, making it an event that could be replicated at will and studied in a laboratory setting.

I found this notion to be very exciting for a number of reasons. First and foremost was that scrying could be a very effective means of grief therapy for patients who were unable to overcome the depression and grief caused by the death of a loved one. Since grief is one of the most difficult of human emotions to overcome, I was particularly interested in this question. Seeing a deceased loved one just one more time could be an important turning point for patients trying to get past their grief and go on with their lives.

I began to write down other reasons why I would launch myself into a study of the unorthodox world of scrying:

Does scrying explain why so many people see ghosts? Excellent medical research had shown that as many as one-fourth of Americans have experienced ghosts at least once, while one-third of Europeans report such experiences. By experiencing ghosts, I don't mean just seeing one but also feeling, hearing, or smelling a ghost. Such encounters are proof that the memories of our loved ones are deeply embedded in our unconscious mind—so deeply that it isn't a great leap to think that we should be able to continue communicating with them in one form or another. Even the late astronomer Carl Sagan, no great fan of paranormal research, wrote in *Parade* magazine about hearing the voices of his parents calling his name more than a dozen times after both had died.

Could crystal gazing make it possible to "see" ghosts in a laboratory setting? Because experiencing ghosts seems to happen spontaneously, there is no methodical way of studying this phenomenon. The study of ghost experiences is just a study of stories about these experiences taking place on their own, with no way of controlling when they occurred. But if crystal gazing was a method of inducing ghost experiences, then they could be created in a laboratory setting and studied by scientists. The idea of being able to observe a person experiencing a ghost was exciting to me. Not only could we observe the brain physiology that allowed this to happen, but we might also be able to investigate any direct connections between the brain and a possible afterlife.

Could crystal gazing make it possible to view the unconscious mind? Since the study of psychology began, researchers like Jung and Freud have insisted that much if not most of what goes on in the human mind takes place in the unconscious. Thus, who we are and how we react and respond to the world is largely invisible and out of our control. Could crystal gazing allow us to *consciously* explore the unconscious, making it visible?

Could crystal gazing make it possible to understand the creative process? Many writers, artists, scientists, and even businessmen credit the unconscious mind as the source of their creativity and their greatest work. Salvador Dali, the surrealist painter, devised methods of wakening himself in the midst of dreams so that he could use their surrealistic qualities on his canvases; the result was melting clocks and other bizarre images. Thomas Edison did the same, using techniques to capture the thoughts in his mind that arose during that fugue state between sleep and wakefulness. Could crystal gazing be a way of tapping into hidden creativity inside each of us? And could the systematic use of crystal gazing overcome blocks to creativity?

Could mirror gazing be a way of exploring interesting and important events in history? The Bible is filled with events that could have been inspired by crystal gazing. In the First Book of Samuel, for instance, King Saul orders all mediums and spiritualists to be expelled from Israel and promises death to anyone who dares to conjure a spirit. Then, in a dramatic turnaround, Saul finds himself in need of advice from the late King Samuel. To avoid looking like a hypocrite, he dresses like a woman and travels to Endor, where a female medium reluctantly conjures the spirit of Samuel. The spirit apparently reveals the true identity of Saul to the medium because she becomes fearful of the king and accuses him of entrapment. Only when he promises to do her no harm does she reveal the spirit of Samuel to King Saul. The king weeps and declares that God no longer speaks to him through "prophets or dreams," so he has now called on the spirit of Samuel to tell him what to do. There are many such events in the Bible as well as throughout history, involving figures like Abraham Lincoln and General George Patton. A study of mirror gazing could reveal some of history's great mysteries.

Is a study of crystal gazing a way to explain humankind's propensity to believe in supernatural forces, or is it a way to actually reach the realm of the supernatural? Studying crystal gazing could reveal for the first time whether a supernatural realm exists by allowing science to re-create ghost experiences and probe them until findings are reached. But does crystal gazing itself open a door into another realm? Is this a door that we could learn to open at will? Would it explain our devout belief in the supernatural?

I hastily jotted down the questions I wanted to answer in my study of crystal gazing and then refined them into the questions listed here. Then I crafted a statement and goal about the work I was about to do that read something like this:

As human beings, we are plagued by fear and anxiety about death.

As a society, we put death in its place, creating cemeteries that keep death out of our view. We have horror films to remind us of the terror in death, but other than that we don't talk about death very much, except when it is required.

In many ways these strictures are aimed at telling us that there is a world of the living and a world of the dead and one side can never venture into the other.

Yet in my experience there is a midway zone between the living and the dead. It is a zone that, logically, has nothing in it.

Without a doubt, there are certain experiences of living consciousness that seem to indicate that we survive death. Near-death experiences are one such phenomenon, as are seeing apparitions of the deceased and shamanic voyages. These experiences are seen as a transition between life and death. Because they have to do with both and yet neither, they might be called adventures of the Middle Realm.

The existence of the Middle Realm has no basis in scientifically proven fact. Yet people of sound mind and good judgment have experiences that convince them that the state of death is a transition into another dimension of awareness called life after death.

With all of this in mind, my goal was to explore mirror visions to see if they might be one way of entering the Middle Realm.

CHAPTER SEVENTEEN

⁓

I was teaching psychology at West Georgia State College at this time and decided to perform a small experiment with the students. I set up a crystal ball in the classroom and had a maintenance worker install light-excluding shades over the windows. I put lit candles around the room for effect. When the students came into the room, I had them sit at the big table around the crystal ball.

A few days earlier I had explained the history and theory of scrying and asked for volunteers for my first experimental session. I didn't want to make participation mandatory for all members of the class, given that some were extremely religious and may have felt that this experiment was akin to devil worship.

Still, the students who had volunteered were somewhat agog when they came into class that day at the way the room had been transformed into a mystical place using only darkness, a few glowing objects, and of course, the enormous crystal ball in the center of the table.

When the students sat down, I did a brief relaxation session with them (which some of the students, who had Deep South sensibilities and weren't accustomed to even the most basic forms of meditation, described as "weird"), and then we began.

The instructions were simple. I told the students to half-close their eyes and gaze into the clear depth of the crystal. Mentally, I said, they should let thoughts pass through their mind until they became empty like blank slates. At that point, I told them, unexpected images might appear. Or they might not.

None of the students saw dead relatives, but a surprising array of images came to them over the one-hour session. Several saw what they believed to be past lives. One student was a soldier in the Civil War, another a nurse in seventeenth-century France, and one white student found himself working hard as an African slave on a southern plantation.

There were other discoveries too. A woman came to my office a few days later and tearfully told me that during the session she had relived childhood molestation by an uncle. And a young man told me privately that he had envisioned being dead and reborn. When he told this to his mother, she confessed that she had indeed left him alone in a bathtub as an infant and found him drowning when she returned. She revived him, but had never told anyone about the incident. He asked me whether I thought this was what he had experienced through scrying.

Based on this simple experiment alone, I could see several therapeutic uses for scrying. Like past-life regressions, scrying seemed to dredge up painful memories, revivifying details and emotions and making them real once again. For patients who were "blocked" about their problems or had perhaps forgotten important details, scrying might be a way to break through these blockages, offering exciting therapeutic possibilities.

But was scrying a means by which to explore the Middle Realm, that place where the living and dying meet during near-death experiences? That question intrigued me, and I began to search for the answer on my own.

In a small closet I devised a simple apparition booth. On one wall I hung a mirror high enough that I could not see myself when I sat down in front of it. The only thing visible would be the clear depth in the mirror as it reflected the wall behind me. Then I installed a twenty-five-watt lightbulb to provide minimal light.

In this simple facility, I became my first experimental subject to attempt a facilitated apparition.

My goal was to see Grandmother Waddleton, my maternal grandmother. In preparation for the experience, I took a long walk and ate a high-carbohydrate breakfast to increase the level of the neurotransmitter serotonin in my bloodstream. Then I spent much of the day looking at photos of my grandmother and remembering her kindness, a wonderful experience.

Then I went into the apparition booth. Sitting in the room's dim light, I gazed into the crystal clear, three-dimensional depth of the offset mirror, which was like looking into a deep mountain lake. I gazed into this mirror for an hour or more, thinking of Grandmother Waddleton and bringing scenes to life from the photos I had looked at for so long.

Yet despite two hours of effort, my beloved grandmother did not appear.

Had I done something wrong? I wondered as I left the booth.

I went downstairs to the living room. It was twilight now, and the experience of scrying had left me surprisingly tired. I remember sitting on the couch, thinking of nothing at all.

Suddenly a woman walked into the room! It took me a moment to realize that this was not my *maternal* grandmother, Grandmother Waddleton, but my *paternal* grandmother, Grandmother Moody, who had died several years earlier.

"Grandma!" I exclaimed, throwing my hands up to my face.

I was awestruck. I had hoped to conjure my maternal grandmother because my memories of her were all very positive. My paternal grandmother was another story. Few of my memories of her were pleasant, and most were distinctly unpleasant. I remembered how she always sided with my father in arguments, and how she washed my mouth with soap for saying a word that she didn't think was appropriate. I even remembered her telling me I'd "go to hell" for flying in an airplane! My memory of her as chronically crabby, however, was in distinct contrast to the woman who was standing before me now, smiling.

We spoke. I heard her, although what I heard came to my ears with a crisp, electric quality that was louder and clearer than her voice had been before she died. Although we spoke and I could hear her, I was immediately aware of what she was saying even before she said it, which has led me to describe this experience as "mind-to-mind" communication.

She did not appear ghostly or transparent but was completely solid. And she was much younger in physical appearance than when she died. In fact, she appeared much younger than I had ever seen her. Still, I recognized her, and I would recognize her today if I saw her on the street. This was my father's mother.

We discussed our family, and she revealed family secrets that I didn't know but that explained many events in my childhood. I choose not to reveal them here, other than to say that these revelations explained some of the dysfunction that has been present in my own life and I have felt better since hearing them from her.

I don't know how long we communicated. It seemed like a couple of hours, but it could also have been just a few seconds. However long it was, the meeting was completely satisfactory, and we wrapped it up in a way that changed my impression of my paternal grandmother. I no longer feared or disliked her.

At the end of our meeting, when there was nothing else to talk about, she said that we would meet again, and I said that I hoped we would. Then I stood up and tried to hug her, but she held up her hands to motion me back. I tried again, and her hands went up again. I noticed that her body was surrounded by a thin line of light that made her stand out from her surroundings; other than that, she looked just like an ordinary person standing there in front of me. I left the room to get a drink of water. When I came back, the apparition was gone.

Everything about the meeting puzzled me. Why did I see my paternal grandmother when I had worked so hard to see my maternal one? Why did she appear to me in the living room after my session in the apparition booth? How was she able to reveal family secrets that I had never known unless she was truly my grandmother?

And so on. The words poured out of me as I wrote them down in one of my ever-present notebooks. I called such experiences "facilitated apparitions," and the excitement I felt over this work came from many different directions. Most important was my continuing study of the ancient Greeks. The ancients constructed psychomanteums all over Greece, and citizens would flock— literally—to these specially designed caves to experience facilitated apparitions. Why did they do that? The most obvious answer was grief therapy. Even the ancients shared the universal desire to spend five more minutes with a departed loved one. If I could replicate the Greeks' method of facilitating apparitions, I could develop a better means of grief therapy.

Developing a controlled method of facilitating apparitions, however, would be far more than just another method of grief therapy: It would be a major step forward in paranormal research. Up until then, apparitional studies had been based on "ghost stories" about events that happen in uncontrolled situations. If apparitions could be facilitated, they could be studied scientifically using a variety of medical and psychological tools. Imagine, for example, a CAT scan image showing exactly how the brain communicates with the Middle Realm!

After a while I put my pen away and mulled over the possibilities. Even though twilight was turning to darkness outside, I knew I was at the dawn of a new adventure.

CHAPTER EIGHTEEN

~

I went in search of the perfect location in which to pursue my study of facilitated apparitions.

I was living in Carrollton, Georgia, at the time and started my search there. My criteria for the right house were simple but expensive. I needed a large place in a quiet neighborhood or perhaps in the country that was surrounded by enough land to give it the feeling of isolation. Being on a creek would be ideal since the sound of running water is relaxing.

The houses being shown to me by the local Realtors that fit these criteria were very expensive. Carrollton was within commuting distance of Atlanta, the Realtors explained, and in recent years city people had been moving here for a small-town experience. Hence, an inexpensive house was not easy to find in Carrollton.

I made my frustrations known to the secretary in the Psychology Department, and she gently offered a solution: Alabama is just eleven miles down the road, she said. Homes are cheaper there.

So I went looking. And it was there that I came to believe that "coincidence" is just another word for universal intention.

Through a friend, I found a beautiful Victorian set in the middle of two acres. I liked what I saw, and soon I was in the office of the real estate agent listed on the FOR SALE sign. I told him who I was and said I wanted to take a look at the Victorian for sale.

The Realtor looked at me slightly askance and said, "What are you really looking for?"

It was a moment of intuition on his part because, although I liked the Victorian, what I really wanted was a gristmill. I had wanted to live in a mill house since I visited one as a young man with my uncle Fairley Waddleton, who was the chief of police of Oxford, Georgia. I had always kept that vision in my mind, and apparently I had it now because the Realtor appeared to know I wanted something different from the Victorian house I came to see him about.

"What are you really looking for?" he repeated.

"I'm a psychiatrist, and I'm looking for a place out in the country where I can do some reading and writing," I said. "My choice would be a gristmill." Naturally, I didn't say anything about gazing into mirrors, and I breathed a sigh of relief when he didn't pick up on that.

He rubbed his chin for a moment and said, "Let me take you to a place near where I live," he said.

We drove down a country road through trees and fields and then over a wooden bridge to a big white gristmill on the edge of a broad and fast-flowing creek. The place was built in 1850, said the Realtor. An identical mill had been built directly across the creek, but it had been burned down in the Civil War. I thought I was in a dream.

"Perfect," I said.

"Yes, it is," he said. "The problem is that it's not for sale."

The house was owned by the Doerrs, who had lived there for decades. Mr. Doerr was a retired sea captain and Mrs. Doerr a retired chemist. The Realtor knew them through their children, who were his age. For some time the children had wanted their parents to move because Mrs. Doerr had arthritis that had worsened from the daily climb up the stairs.

"I'll call them," said the Realtor. "Maybe they'll change their mind about selling."

When the Realtor called, he made his pitch to Mrs. Doerr. She made it clear that they weren't interested in selling. "But you can show the house anyway," she said.

I was on my best behavior that day as we knocked on the front door and went inside. I held out my hand to Mrs. Doerr and introduced myself.

"Dr. Raymond Moody," she said, her eyes looking off in the distance. "Dr. Raymond Moody . . . Dr. Raymond Moody. . . . Are you the man who wrote that book?"

Before I could answer, she walked into the living room and pulled a book off the shelf next to the fireplace. It wasn't my book at all, but a book by Dr. George Ritchie, the good friend to whom I had dedicated my first book, *Life After Life*. I had also written the foreword for Ritchie's book, and that's what she was enthusiastically pointing at now.

"George Ritchie is one of our dear, dear friends," she said. "I think this must be a sign."

The chances of finding a gristmill that someone was willing to sell was highly unlikely, but the idea that they would be connected to me in any way, let alone through my good friend George Ritchie, was beyond belief for me.

Within a month I was in the home of my dreams.

I brought in a local contractor who altered one of the upstairs rooms to my specifications, and soon I had my own psychomanteum.

My goal, of course, was to answer one question: Can apparitions of deceased loved ones be consistently facilitated in normal, healthy people?

I devised simple criteria for the test subjects I would assemble:

- They must be mature people interested in human consciousness.

- They must be emotionally stable, inquisitive, and articulate.

- None of the subjects could have emotional or mental disorders.

- None of the subjects could have occult ideologies, since such leanings could complicate the analysis of the results.

With these criteria in mind, I contacted ten subjects and asked if they would like to participate in my "Reunions Experiment."

During a ten-day period, I scheduled each subject for a one-day session. Each one arrived on his or her appointed day, bearing mementos and photo albums of the person they hoped to see. They all dressed in comfortable clothing and had eaten a light breakfast with no caffeine drinks so they could relax.

I started each session with a leisurely walk in the countryside, exploring the person's motivation for attempting to see the departed. I told each subject that there were no guarantees of seeing the departed loved one, but that we would try.

After the walk, we would eat a light lunch of soup, salad, and fruit and then discuss in detail the person who had died and the subject's relationship with that person.

Usually the subject would bring up touching memories. Often these memories would receive a boost from the mementos, which had been set between us. One man brought his father's fishing equipment. A woman brought her sister's hat. Another subject had his father's war medals. All were poignant and tangible reminders of the deceased.

Sometimes I would have the subject lie on a bed that had been built by a staff member. The bed was equipped with speakers, and the music emanating from them could be felt via bone conduction throughout the body.

These preparatory sessions lasted until dusk. Then, at the mystical hour of sunset, I would escort the subject into the mirror-gazing booth and turn on the electric light that was only as bright as a single candle. I would tell the subject to gaze deeply into the mirror and relax, clearing his or her mind of everything but thoughts of the deceased. Subjects could stay in the room as long as they wanted, but I asked them to refrain from wearing a watch so that they would not be tempted to glance at the time.

An attendant sat in the next room during the entire session in case any assistance was required. When the subject emerged, I encouraged discussion of what had happened for as long as the subject desired. Some of these debriefing sessions went on for longer than an hour. I made it a point not to hurry them. The session was not over until the subject decided it was over.

I had some assumptions before starting this research. I expected that only one or two of the subjects would actually see a dead relative. And I suspected that those subjects who did experience an apparition would doubt the reality of what they saw.

The picture that emerged was vastly different from what I expected. Of the ten pioneers ushered through this process, five had powerful apparitions of dead relatives. And all of them believed that they had actually seen their departed loved one and communicated with that person.

The first subject's experience is still the most amazing to me because it showed that my technique truly worked, although in this case it worked in an unexpected way.

I will call this first subject Ruth. She was a forty-four-year-old nurse whose husband had died two years earlier of a heart attack. She prepared to see him by following my suggestion that she bring along a photo album of their marriage and several mementos. We spent several hours talking about Ruth's husband and preparing her to see him, but when she came out of the mirror-gazing booth, she told me with great bewilderment that she had seen her father instead of her husband, and that "Dad" had actually emerged from the mirror to talk with her.

Another of these early patients went *into* the mirror and arrived at a structure that was like a "railway platform," where he met with his two cousins who had died. He was puzzled as he talked about what he had seen. "It seemed as though they were waiting for me," he said. Coincidentally (or not), this patient died a few months later in an automobile accident.

Another woman came to see her late grandmother, who not only appeared in the mirror and stepped out into the gazing booth but also put her arms around her granddaughter and warmly hugged her.

An East Coast surgeon came to see his late mother, to whom he felt he owed a great debt of gratitude for his success. She appeared to him in the mirror, where she was sitting on a couch. They had a wordless conversation, one that took place through mental communications.

"Was there any pain when you died?" he asked her.

"None at all," she said. "The transition was easy."

He continued.

"What do you think of the woman I am going to marry?"

"It will be a very good choice," she answered, once again wordlessly. "You should continue to work hard at the relationship and not be your old self. Try to be more understanding."

After about ten questions, the surgeon's mother faded away. It was a very emotional time for this man, who felt he had dipped into a realm that he had only heard about and never truly believed existed until now.

I too was stunned at the results as I realized that the psychomanteum offered an exciting form of grief therapy. Instead of having to talk to a therapist about the loss of a loved one, a person in the psychomanteum could talk directly to the loved one.

Visionary encounters with departed loved ones are not frightening. On the contrary, they tend to be positive experiences that give people hope and a sense that the departed is comfortable, happy, and still with them spiritually. I knew this through my work in near-death studies. People who have near-death experiences are less afraid during the experience if they encounter a departed loved one. These encounters are just one of several factors that transform NDEers' lives by making them less afraid of death.

I was thrilled at the notion that I could facilitate these pow-
erfully transformative meetings in the Middle Realm. But I was
also thrilled that I had been able to reveal in living detail the role
of the Oracles in ancient Greece. Without understanding the
role of the Oracles, it is impossible to understand Greek culture.
It was the Oracle at Delphi that declared Socrates to be the smart-
est man in history, a declaration that set him on a lifelong search
for meaning and understanding. The teaching center of Pythago-
ras was modeled after the Oracles, as were the teaching centers
of other wise men from this amazing era. Many of these teaching
centers—places where people could delve into their own psyches—
were also known as psychomanteums.

Yet despite the fact that psychomanteums played such a large
role in ancient Greek culture, little was known about them until
late in the twentieth century. Historians like E. R. Dodds, who
wrote *The Greeks and the Irrational*, said that the psychomanteums
were caves where the teachers of the time called up the dead. But
how or why was not known.

That all changed in the mid-1980s when archaeologist Sotirios
Dakaris searched for and discovered the most famous Oracles of
the Dead. His book revealed that he had discovered warrens of
tunnels with dark corridors that led to underground chambers
illuminated with torches. In one of the Oracles he and his team
found a large copper cauldron that could hold a clear depth of
steaming water in which a person could gaze and see those who
had gone before.

By reading the Greek magical papyri, scrolls of magical reci-
pes found in Egypt but written in Greek, I could tell how the
ancients achieved a magical solution to problems ranging from
getting rid of an enemy to finding the love of one's life. And of
course, talking to departed loved ones.

Fill a bowl with water and cover it with a layer of olive oil, reads one prescription. Then surround the bowl with candles and chant these magical words (which are essentially nonsensical words aimed at clearing one's mind) and wait for the departed to appear.

By following the instructions of the magical papyri in a facility designed for just this purpose, I had created a modern psychomanteum in the style of the ancient Greeks.

Being an obsessive-compulsive personality, I dove into what I was now calling the "Reunions Project," dedicated to achieving a gateway to the psyche. The biggest motivator for me in creating a psychomanteum was to deepen my understanding of the ancient Greeks, a culture I truly respected because it was based largely on the pursuit of knowledge. I called my psychomanteum "the John Dee Theater of the Mind," naming it for the mathematical genius who was the official scryer (crystal gazer) for Queen Elizabeth I. I put out a call for patients.

And the patients came.

Through word of mouth, people found out about the Theater of the Mind and began arriving from all over the country, and then from all over the world. Soon I was overbooked with people who wanted to see their late loved ones.

I had clearly underestimated the appeal of the psychomanteum. I began to imagine that my rural Theater of the Mind would be like the ancient Greek Oracles, which attracted thousands of people each year who were so driven to see the departed that they traveled to the Oracles on foot. They often waited outside for days, camping in primitive conditions or renting local rooms, before being admitted to the heavily populated caves.

I feared that my modern-day Oracle would be no different.

Soon the patient load became overwhelming, and I became overwhelmed. Because the psychomanteum was still in its experimental phase, I wanted to manage every aspect of the reunion experience. That meant devoting all of my energy to only one patient each day—an exhausting prospect considering that most of them were in a fragile emotional condition. Sometime these sessions would go on late into the night and be followed the next day by a session with another person just as emotionally needy. Soon I was on a treadmill of work, and that played havoc with my myxedema, which never seemed to fully go away, even with careful administration of medication.

All that kept me going were the case studies, which provided fascinating confirmation of the effectiveness and value of this modern version of a technique practiced so effectively by the Greeks. I conducted more than one hundred patients through the psychomanteum in the first months of the Theater of the Mind and was able to explore the varieties of experience that patients had when we used these amazing techniques.

Many people had an encounter with a deceased person other than the one they had intended to see. I figured that about one-fourth of the patients visited with someone unexpected—sometimes very unexpected. Also, many apparitions were not confined to the mirror but came out to be with the person. When this happened, patients often reported either being "touched" by the apparition or being able to feel its presence.

One example came from a man who prepared all day to see his father, who had died when the subject was only twelve years old. After hours of preparation, the man was surprised to be greeted in the mirror by his former business partner, a person he didn't even particularly like. Here is his account of what followed:

When he came into the apparition booth, I saw him clearly. He was about two feet away from me. I was so surprised I couldn't think what to do. It was him, right there. He was my size, and I saw him from the waist up. He had a full form and was not transparent. He moved around, and when he did I could see his head and arms move, all in three dimensions.

He was happy to see me. I was amazed, but he didn't seem amazed. He knew what was going on, was my impression. He wanted to reassure me. He was telling me not to worry, that he was fine. I know that his thought was that we would be together again. His wife is dead now too, and he was sending me the thought that she was with him, but for some reason I was not supposed to see her.

I asked him several questions. I wanted to know something about his daughter that had always concerned me. I had kept in touch with three of his children and helped them out. But there was some difficulty with his second daughter. I had reached out to her, but she blamed me to some extent for her father's death. As she grew older, she said we had worked too hard. So I asked him what to do, and he gave me complete reassurance about what I wanted to know, and it cleared some things up for me.

Without question, this man felt that his business partner had come out of the mirror to sit with him. It allowed him to make peace with his partner and "put to rest" his worries about his partner's family.

About half of the patients reported communicating with the person who appeared in the mirror. And approximately 15 percent of those who successfully saw a person in the mirror said that they also heard the voice of the deceased person—not the *thoughts* of the deceased, but that person's actual, audible voice.

And then there were the "take-out" visions, apparitions that took place later, after the patient had left the psychomanteum. Roughly 25 percent of those who came seeking reunions had them *after* they had left the gazing booth and returned home or to their hotel. One such case was a well-respected television journalist who saw nothing in the mirror but did see her son, who had committed suicide, several hours later at the hotel. Here is what she had to say:

When I got back to the hotel where I was staying, I made a few phone calls. Then I went to bed and fell sound asleep.

I don't know exactly what time it was that I woke up, but when I did I felt a presence in the room, and there was this young man standing in the room, between the television set and the dresser.

At first he was pretty expressionless, and he was looking at me. I was so frightened, my heart was going a hundred miles a minute. I am glad I was in a king-size bed because I think I would have fallen off the bed, I was so scared.

What was going through my mind was, *Oh God, there must be another entrance to the room!* That's how real he was, standing there.

This was no dream. I was wide awake. I saw him clearly, his whole body, except I didn't see his face. I looked at him, and he looked at me. I don't know how long it was, but it was long enough for me to be frightened, and I don't frighten easily.

But then I realized that I was having an apparition, that this was my son. It didn't look like him at first, but putting everything together, I realized it was him. As a matter of fact, it looked exactly like him as he had looked about ten years earlier.

It became very peaceful after that. I was very assured about my son, that he is okay and that he loves me. This was a turning point for me. It was a wonderful experience.

Most interesting to me was the change that came over the people who had an apparition experience. Almost all of them defined their reunion as being "real," meaning that it was not a fantasy or dream. Because they knew their experience was real, the subjects came away with a different outlook on life. As a result of seeing a being they thought had been extinguished by death, they became kinder, more understanding, and much less afraid of death.

In short, they became just like people who had had a near-death experience, only they didn't have to almost die to get there.

CHAPTER NINETEEN

⁓

It didn't take me long to realize that I had made a major breakthrough in near-death studies. By melding ancient and modern techniques, I had discovered how to arouse many of the transformative elements of the near-death experience in people who were not near death. It was a great leap forward in the field, because controlled studies had been impossible up to that point. Plus, these techniques would provide a means of studying apparitions on a variety of levels, allowing for the examination of everything related to ghosts.

I now understood on an even deeper level the words of the great psychologist William James when he said: "The subliminal life has windows of outlook and doors of ingress which indefinitely extend the region of the world of truth."

Over the year that I conducted almost daily scrying sessions, I wrote copious notes. Now I compiled those notes into a lecture paper for a European tour that had been arranged for me. Fully expecting criticism, I decided that the only way I could stave off a wave of ridicule would be to provide information that was perfectly logical.

I began my paper by explaining exactly what scrying is, how I had discovered it, and its effect on me. Then I discussed the ancient Greeks and described their use of scrying in the Oracles they called psychomanteums. Apparently this was an effective means of therapy for grief and other issues because in ancient Greece thousands of people each year spent weeks underground in hopes of traveling to the Middle Realm.

I described how I established a modern-day psychomanteum in a country home and how I altered a room with mirrors and dim lights to inspire the correct frame of mind in the patients. With the help of remembrance, focus, and deep relaxation, I noted, patients could then voyage to a Middle Realm that until then had been accessible only in the stories and myths of ancient Greece.

I provided several stories from the psychomanteum and revealed the discoveries that I have revealed in this book—that the deceased sometimes come out of the mirror, or that patients sometimes see someone other than the person they expected to see.

In the paper, I declared that what was important were not the specific stories, but rather the realization that these experiences could be controlled and so studied in a clinical setting. "Mirror gazing may well finally allow these altered states to be studied in a laboratory setting," I wrote. "This would represent a major leap forward in psychology. It would mean subjects could be interviewed immediately after—or even during—an altered state."

I suggested that electroencephalograms and positron-emission tomography could be carried out during an apparitional experience to map the metabolic activity in the brain during these encounters. Perhaps then we could find "hard links" in the brain that would help us explore afterlife questions.

"Up until now it has been impossible to investigate these altered states in a laboratory," I wrote.

Because of that, many skeptics have said that those who have paranormal experiences as well as those who research them tend to "overstate" what happens, or even that the experiences themselves are fabricated by the subjects. This uninformed opinion rarely takes into consideration the sheer masses of people who see ghosts, or have near-death experiences, or even leave their bodies. Although we are talking about millions of people in these categories, some cynics call them liars or crackpots, denying an experience that they should instead be investigating. Mirror gazing would allow legitimate researchers an opportunity to research the outer reaches of the mind, and to show once and for all if they truly exist.

Although I endorsed the use of crystal gazing, or scrying, as a research tool, I wrote that my main interests lay in the clinical uses of this ancient art. In working closely with people seeking reunion with departed loved ones, I could see firsthand how this tool was helping patients.

I closed the paper for my European lecture tour with the story of a woman who came to the psychomanteum for a visionary reunion with her son who had died two years earlier of cancer. He had fought hard against the disease, but every time he was bolstered by a remission, the disease would come charging back, taking the old ground and then a little more. Finally he gave up.

The woman missed her son terribly and came to the psycho-manteum in hopes of seeing him one more time. She wanted to know if the pain was gone and if he was happy in the afterlife.

We prepared all day for the encounter, and then I had her go into the apparition booth. She relived a number of memory snip-pets, dreamlike memories from his childhood. She also reported that he seemed to be in the booth with her, watching their life together.

And that was it. Until a few days later. Then I received an incredible telephone call from her. A few days after her visit to my clinic, she awoke from a deep sleep into a state of "hyper-awareness."

There, standing in the room, was her son. She sat up in bed and looked at him. The ravages of cancer were gone. He now looked as happy and healthy as he had been before the cancer that took him.

The woman stood before her son and began carrying on a con-versation. She was in a state of ecstasy as they spoke for several minutes. He assured her that he was pain-free and happy.

The woman continued to engage him in a conversation about a number of things, including the remodeling she had done to the house after he died. She took him on a tour of the rooms that had been changed and showed him what she had done.

Suddenly she stopped. She realized that she was talking to an apparition. And even though he seemed to be flesh and bone, he had come to her as a result of a lot of time spent before a mirror. She asked what had been unthinkable just a few minutes earlier. She asked if she could touch him.

Without a moment's hesitation, the apparition of her son stepped forward and hugged her, lifting her right off the ground.

"What happened was as real as if he had been standing right

there," the woman told me. "I now feel as though I can put my son's death behind me and get on fully with my life."

Reactions like this are the real reason I work on the fringes of psychological sciences, I would tell my European audiences. I appreciate the test tubes and research protocol, but there is something about witnessing the raw experience that compels me to continue my exploration into near-death studies.

This, in a nutshell, was the core of my lecture for the European tour. When I began it, I was deeply concerned that I might be laughed off the stage by talking about mirror gazing. So far I had spoken about it to only a few professionals in the United States. For the most part they had listened politely but were not wildly enthusiastic, especially when they realized the amount of time it took to treat one patient. By prescribing medications, a psychiatrist could treat a couple dozen patients per day. Even traditional talk therapy allowed them to jam in eight to ten patients a day. But by using the methods outlined in my reunions therapy, they could treat only one. It's nearly impossible to get an American psychiatrist enthused about treating one patient per day, especially using a time-intensive regimen that would require them to pay careful attention to the patient all day long. Plus, it was an innovative therapy. Which insurance company would pay for that?

I didn't expect the response to my reunions work to be much greater in Europe, but I was wrong. The doctors there were outwardly intrigued by the possibilities of what I presented to them. Liberal-minded when it came to new psychological treatments, the audiences were curious and filled with questions? Were patients frightened when they saw their departed loved ones? Did having these experiences make people happier about life, or unhappier? Did departed relatives who had done bad things ever appear and apologize? And if so, did that solve any issues the living person might have with the dead one? Could scrying be done in groups as effectively as with individuals?

The questions just kept coming. My lecture would typically last about one hour, but the question-and-answer session at the end would sometimes go on for twice that long. Their questions kept coming. What is the success rate? And how do you define success? Are some of these experiences unpleasant for the subjects? Have you ever done scrying with an atheist? Do you even have to believe in God to believe in an afterlife?

After each lecture I would receive offers to establish temporary clinics in which I could return to the city for several months per year and practice. There were many who saw, as I did, that this line of research could take the murkiness out of paranormal studies. They saw this as a way to study the meaning and validity of apparitions and offered to find institutions that would offer facilities and funds to do research.

I was delighted at the positive response. But I was also exhausted. Several weeks before leaving the United States, my thyroid level had plunged to a dangerous low. I had gone to my doctor, who brought my levels back up, but that was never an indication that they would stay up where they should be. I was like a brittle diabetic whose blood insulin levels could take wild swings. For the time being I was fine, said my internist. But he warned me that with all the work I had been doing, the airplane travel, and the frigid weather I would encounter in Europe, I would probably have a wild "thyroxin ride" on my lecture tour.

My doctor's weather warming was well heeded. In warm weather I had to take far less thyroxin than when it was cold. He adjusted me for the warmer Alabama weather but reminded me to stay on top of my levels in Europe. "Remember, Raymond, you don't have a thyroid gland," warned my doctor. "So you are always on one side of the line or the other. Try to stay as close to the line as you can. Keep your thyroid levels stable."

My plan to stay close to the line was simple. I would go into a local hospital or clinic and have them test my thyroid level. Then I would take medications accordingly.

Unfortunately, things didn't work as I planned. Toward the middle of my tour, I was in Czechoslovakia when I began to feel goofy. I was concerned about going to a clinic in the Czech Republic and being stuck with a needle. I had heard that many Eastern Bloc countries were reusing needles as a means of saving money, and I didn't want to run the risk of being exposed to AIDS, hepatitis C, or any variety of the other blood-borne diseases.

Rather, I crushed my pills and took them in crumb-sized bites, hoping that the small doses would raise my thyroid level enough that I could wait until I got to Switzerland, where medical care was better. I was doing two lectures per day now, with no days off and seemingly no time to get a blood test, let alone wait for the results. Or so I thought.

In fact, I should have made time, but I didn't. I was exhausted, delusional, and forgetful. Looking back, I don't remember much of that last week or so of the tour. I do remember thinking that I had my thyroid issues under control and then feeling a deep fear that I didn't, but pressing on anyway. The adrenaline of the tour would replace thyroid medicine, I told myself.

Sometimes our denial can lead us to become our own worst enemies.

CHAPTER TWENTY

~

By the time I returned from my European tour, I was desperately ill from myxedema. I was cold to the bone all the time, and the man who greeted me in the mirror had sagging skin and a gray complexion. At times I felt as though I was looking at an alien. I had that detached feeling, like I was watching a movie instead of living my life. That movie was slowly turning to black-and-white as my color vision began shutting down from the critically low level of thyroid in my bloodstream.

I simply needed rest until the medication took hold and raised my thyroid level. I needed a warm bed and the comforts of home. I needed my mother and father. I needed to go back to Macon, Georgia, where they lived. I needed family.

When I arrived home, my father was obviously disturbed at the way I looked. He asked me where I'd been, and when I told him I was lecturing in Europe, he asked me what about.

"I'm sharing my psychomanteum research," I said.

"What's that?" he asked, concern clearly filling his voice.

Uh oh, I thought. I had not told him anything at all about my scrying work and research, and now I could tell he was alarmed.

"Oh, it's some techniques from the ancient Greeks," I mumbled, trying to avoid conversation.

"What *kind* of techniques?" he asked, gazing with an intense skepticism he reserved only for me.

"Oh, you know, Greeks spent sometimes weeks in an underground labyrinth before entering a large room and gazing into a cauldron of water where they would then see dead relatives," I mumbled, reciting by rote portions of the lectures I had delivered in Europe. "They were called Oracles of the Dead."

"So what does this have to do with you?" my father asked, the note of concern in his voice now intensifying.

"I've figured out a way to modernize it," I said, all the while drifting around in that blue-and-gray netherworld of myxedema. "I've created techniques that get people in the right frame of consciousness to see their dead loved ones."

"You what?"

"Yes, and then I have developed a chamber where they can gaze into an off-kilter mirror and see their dead relatives," I said.

"You have?!"

"Yes, and the whole technique can be very effective. Some of the patients have even had their dead relatives come out of the mirror and sit with them in conversation," I said, a little more excited. "Some of the patients have even had their dead relatives appear later, after they have left the psychomanteum."

"Psychomanteum?"

"Yes, 'psychomanteum' is what I call the chamber where they sit and gaze into the mirror."

My father seemed genuinely interested as I told him about patients who had experienced successful grief therapy through the psychomanteum. When I got to the story about the woman whose dead son had hugged her so hard that her feet left the floor, he got up and left the room.

Many minutes later he came back and put his hand on my forehead. I was stone cold. He listened to my heart with a stethoscope, stuck a tongue depressor into my mouth, and then shined a light into my eyes to gauge the reaction of my pupil to light.

"You need to go to the hospital," he stated authoritatively.

"Yes, I do," I said. "I am not feeling well."

He left the room again, and in no time at all men in white coats came in and helped me to my feet. The world through my eyes was gray now, and I was thrilled to be going to the hospital. I had no fear that I would be stuck with a dirty needle here in the United States. Rather than having to guess how much thyroid medication I should take, medical tests could pinpoint the exact amount.

I thanked the men in white coats for helping me, and I thanked my father for calling them. I didn't see Mom, but I could hear her sobbing in the kitchen.

"Tell Mom I'll be okay pretty soon," I said to my father. I was looking forward to coming back home when my Technicolor world returned.

The ambulance ride was a little foggy to me, but it wasn't long before I realized that we were not headed for Macon General Hospital.

"Where are we going?" I asked one of the white coats.

He ignored me, and I went to sleep.

. . .

We're here," said one of the white coats, shaking me gently. I opened my eyes to see that the hospital my father had in mind was one specializing in psychiatric disorders.

I was angry and puzzled. My father was such a well-respected physician in Georgia that he was able to have his son committed to an institution just because he didn't understand the research and work I had been doing and thought I was delusional. *Certainly the admitting doctor will understand and order me sent to the regular hospital,* I thought as I was escorted into the facility by the white coats on each of my arms. After all, I had just spent a month in Europe lecturing. I had been received with standing ovations from medical doctors, many of whom wanted to come to the United States and learn the techniques of the psychomanteum. Surely this doctor would recognize the value of my work as, at the very least, a holistic approach to grief treatment. I expected to have a good laugh with the admitting physician over the fact that an old doctor had committed a young one for pursuing an ancient form of medicine.

It was soon clear that the laugh would be on me.

I was escorted to a small office and greeted by a cheerless physician I'll call Dr. Hoot, who introduced himself as a board-certified psychiatrist. He began to ask questions about my mental state and soon clearly understood that I had myxedema and that I needed to get my circulating thyroid to its proper level. All was proceeding well, I thought, as the doctor took notes and I recited my glandular problems as I had to other physicians so many times before.

By now I had been at the hospital several hours, and my son Avery had arrived after being notified of the situation by his grandmother. Suddenly I remembered that I was to make a presentation of my psychomanteum work the very next month at Carlton College in Minnesota. They were waiting for information about my upcoming talk so they could publicize the event in a brochure that would be sent to the student body. I reached into my briefcase and pulled out a few pages that described the ancient history of the Oracles of the Dead and my modern approach to facilitating apparitions.

Before giving these pages to Avery so he could take them home and fax them to Carlton, I asked Dr. Hoot if he could make an extra copy. After an uncomfortably long time, Dr. Hoot returned and handed the original to me and a copy to Avery. He had a look on his face that immediately told me I had made a mistake in handing him the document.

"I hope you don't mind, but I took the liberty of making a copy for myself," he said. "This clearly shows that you have gone over the edge. Gazing in mirrors to see spirits? This clearly shows that you are a manic-depressive and need more than a dose of thyroid medication."

He then tried to convince me to take lithium, a powerful drug used in the treatment of manic depression. Although he prescribed the mind-numbing drug, I refused to take it. Instead, I insisted that they treat the myxedema.

That turned out to be the right thing to do, because my health took a nosedive within the next twenty-four hours. Thyroid functions in the body in much the same way as the volume dial on a radio. When turned to the correct level, the human organism functions just fine. But if the level of thyroid is too low, every aspect of the body functions poorly or not at all. My thyroid level was rapidly depleting, and as it did my volume dial was going down and down. My world went from gray to grayer to nearly black. I no

longer worried about which hospital I was in, but was just glad to
be in any hospital. When I could think at all, I began to think that
I might not survive.

On my third day in the hospital I began to sense that I was
surrounded by some very strong beings. They weren't angels, not
even close, but they were otherworldly. They seemed very real.

I never did see these people, but they were there, hovering
around, apparently waiting to see if I was going to die. They were
not menacing. Quite the opposite. If I had to give them a name it
would be "the Tough Love Crew." They counseled me not through
words but through heart-to-heart communications. They didn't
know if I was going to die, they said, but they told me not to worry,
that it didn't matter one way or the other. Dead or alive, it was all
the same.

Then it was as though the physical layer of life fell away and I
was in a parallel layer occupied by these beings. I was very conscious of this new realm because it was almost like being backstage at a play. I had a sense that real life was the play going on out
there on the stage and that it was being controlled backstage. Being there made reality seem almost meaningless. The colors I saw
were very vibrant, and the light seemed alive with substance and
information. Anything I wanted to know was right there when I
wanted it. I could pose questions to these people through the light
and they would respond.

I asked a question about suicide: Was it ever necessary? One of
the female entities answered that it was never necessary to commit suicide because earthly problems are never as meaningful as
they seem.

"Earthly things seem to have so much foreboding when we are
on earth, but once you leave it you realize how small earthly problems are," she said. This woman, when alive, had once worked

in a tax assessor's office, she said. Since I was having financial problems at this time, I asked her what to do. She dismissed my problems as meaningless in the grand scale of things. "Money is nothing," she said, and let it go at that.

The experience in the hospital grew. I realized that Vi Horton, one of the first near-death experiencers I had ever met, was sitting at the foot of my bed. Oddly enough, I was not surprised to see Vi, who had had one of the most profound and verifiable near-death experiences I had ever studied: She had gone into cardiac arrest on the operating table and left her body. In this state, she drifted into the hospital waiting room and later was able to tell surprised family members what they had said as they waited for word from the doctor.

Vi didn't know that I was now in the hospital. A few weeks later, when the ordeal was finally over, I visited her in Augusta and told her that I had been hospitalized. She interrupted me and said, "Yes, I know that, and I had an out-of-body experience and was there with you." She even told me the location of the hospital and which room I had been in.

Some medical professionals who have heard me speak of these bizarre events say that I was merely delirious. But I have been delirious a few times in my life, and I can tell you that this was a completely different experience. Delirium is patchy and confused, and the imagery is surrealistically distorted. This was not like that. The imagery was more real and coherent than the ordinary physical reality we live in.

It was certainly more coherent than the one I found myself in when the thyroid medication took hold. When that happened, I found myself leaving that gray place and heading back to the Technicolor world. I was eating again, being able to taste food, and seeing colors, and best of all, I was ready for exercise.

When not in the hospital, I walk several miles each day. Now, feeling exercise-deprived, I received permission to work out on the exercise bicycle in the hospital gymnasium. One day I was pedaling hard when a well-meaning nurse approached and asked if I thought I should be doing that. She had looked at my chart and seen the notes of Dr. Hoot. Believing I was manic-depressive—which was what Dr. Hoot had wrongly put in my record—the nurse was concerned that I might be in a manic mood and exercising too much.

The fact was, however, that they had taken my ordinary behavior and fit it into symptoms of manic depression. And since I exercise a lot, my good exercise habits were now considered a part of the wrong diagnosis. It was frustrating for me to carry this diagnosis, since it affected the way everyone saw and dealt with me. I soon became known to the staff as the noncompliant manic-depressive, the one who would not take his lithium.

I think they would have forced me to take lithium had I not so obviously been improving as a result of the thyroid medication. Dr. Hoot seemed almost disappointed that I had so quickly become my old self again. He strongly recommended that I take the lithium at first but gradually said little about it as I began to resemble a warm-blooded animal instead of the reptilian creature that myxedema can turn me into.

Then, as friends and patients heard I was in the hospital, they began to drop by to see how I was doing. They talked to Dr. Hoot and told him that, yes, they were familiar with my psychomanteum research and, yes, it actually worked. Some of them told the doubting doctor how they had been helped in their battle against grief by experiencing a facilitated apparition of a loved one. I watched Dr. Hoot listen in disbelief as one patient told of her late son, a suicide, who had appeared in full body form and carried on a conversation that gave her closure and changed her life.

I finally had the opportunity to talk to Dr. Hoot in private about my facilitated apparition research. I can say that he never truly appreciated my research, which was okay with me. The Oracles of the Dead and psychomanteums aren't the kind of thing that some doctors even care to understand. But as I told Dr. Hoot, they were the kind of thing that all doctors should at least be aware of, if for no other reason than that such knowledge would increase their understanding of the reach of the human mind.

I didn't tell him to avoid making snap diagnoses about patients by assuming that everyone fits nicely into one diagnostic pattern or another. I wanted to, but held back. That was something he should have learned in medical school.

CHAPTER TWENTY-ONE

ᕜ

Less than a year after this unpleasantness with my father and the mental hospital, I was interviewed on television by the girl of my dreams. Her name was Cheryl Marks, and she was a television producer and talk show host at WTOG in Tampa, Florida. Cheryl had lost her husband some years earlier. When she had a spontaneous apparitional experience with him not long after his death, she became passionately interested in near-death studies and my reunions work.

We were attracted like magnets from the day of the interview onward. A year later, in the fall of 1993, we married, and Cheryl moved to the Theater of the Mind in Alabama. It never ceases to amaze me how life unfolds. In the midst of some of my darkest depressions, I met the light of my life. Within a decade we would adopt two children from very different cultures. Carter, a Mexican child from a U.S. border town, came to us in 1998, and Carol

Ann, a Blackfeet Indian from Montana, came in 2000. Having them has been a dream come true.

Four years before the children arrived, however, and one year after we married, Cheryl and I took a belated honeymoon to Greece, where our goal was to see the Oracles of the Dead.

We hit the main tourist sites for a few days, but then went north to a place called Loannina so we could visit the nearby Oracle of the Dead in a place called Kanalaki.

The Oracle itself was high on a hill outside the town of Kanalaki. We took an eight-mile cab ride to get there. When we drove up the winding dirt road to the entrance, there was no ticket booth and no one at all in sight, let alone anyone from the Greek Antiquities Department. The sign on the gate said that the hours were 10:00 to 4:00, so we told the cab driver to return for us at closing, and we let him drive away.

That was when we met Socrates.

The first we saw of Socrates was his gnarled hand emerging from a cave near the entrance to the Oracle complex. Then the man himself appeared, a rugged, slightly heavy brute with longish unkempt hair and a lengthy beard peppered with gray. He was the ugliest person I'd seen in some time. He was surprised to see us, and he let us know in heavily accented English. "No one ever comes here, least of all Americans," he said.

He gave us a tour of the roughly excavated Oracle site. We could still see the roof tiles of the Oracles and the excavated walls that marked the residences of the priests who facilitated the visions. Off to one side were walls that revealed a larger complex that Socrates said had housed the hotel rooms where visitors would wait their turn before going down into the tunnels.

When we got to the niches in the caves where the patients slept, Socrates insisted that we lie down and take a nap. "It's the only real way to appreciate the dream incubation that went on here," he declared.

We slept for about an hour and were awakened by Socrates. He wanted to take us through the rest of the complex. First, he said, each of us had to throw a rock over one shoulder, the ancient gesture for leaving one's past behind. With that ritual behind us, we went deeper into one of the tunnels. In the dark he held forth as if teaching a class, walking us through the entire procedure used to invoke the spirits of departed loved ones—the same procedure I used in Alabama.

"I was an attendant here 2,300 years ago," he said, mixing English, Greek, and German. "I know how it's done."

Cheryl didn't like Socrates and was glad when we left. She caught him leering lasciviously at her several times, and he kept saying she reminded him of Melina Mercouri, Greece's sultry version of Marilyn Monroe. On the other hand, I was intrigued by Socrates. There are few people in the world who understand how the Oracles of the Dead work.

I returned to the Oracle site a year later with filmmaker David Hinshaw. We were working on a documentary about the Oracles, and this was one we had chosen to include.

This time we were greeted by a young man instead of Socrates. He spoke very good English and allowed us to roam and film freely. As we left I asked the smiling young man what had happened to Socrates. He became very serious.

"What do you mean?" he asked.

"The man who used to work here," I said. "I met him when we were here last year."

The young man shrugged. He was clearly uncomfortable.

"Other people have met the Socrates you talk about too," he said. "But I have never met him. I think he comes only to certain people."

I don't know that I believe the Socrates we saw was an apparition. He seemed very real to both of us. But when I look back on the experience of meeting Socrates, I realize that it's impossible to study ancient Greek philosophy without acknowledging the role of the Oracles. The mission in life of the real Socrates was started when he was told at an Oracle site that he was the wisest man. That led him to ask his famous questions of intelligent people, and ever since other Greek scholars have been seeking answers to difficult questions.

Because of that, the Oracles of the Dead are an unknown yet very important part of Western thought. With my scrying experiments, I was hoping to bring this concept back into the public arena, making it an important holistic treatment for grief as well as a method of personal exploration, if nothing else.

That has happened to some extent. Over the years since developing modern techniques for scrying, I have had the opportunity to teach these techniques around the world to many therapists who now use them with great effectiveness. But I have also faced the reality of our modern times: We are a pharmaceutical culture, one that would rather use pills to tackle problems like grief than invest the substantial amount of time and energy it takes to have a visionary encounter with a loved one.

I understand why most people would choose to deaden grief rather than resolve it. Some people just don't know about these techniques, others might think they are not in keeping with the culture of their religion, and still others are convinced that they are not effective or unmotivated to explore them themselves.

I also understand why a pharmaceutical approach to grief appeals to people in my profession. The techniques I have described in these chapters are extremely time-consuming and exhausting for the practitioner, as I have personally discovered. My reunions work made me much busier than I wanted to be.

But to me the thrill of inquiry is in discovering new things. And that's how it was in the beginning with the mirror gazing. As long as I was doing it with faculty members, medical colleagues, students, and others in a controlled group of people, there were no expectations. They knew they were part of an experimental group and were willing to accept any outcome.

When actual patients came into the picture, they often misunderstood what was going on. Rather than thinking of me as the facilitator of an experience, they started treating me like a magician, as though I were in charge of whether they saw a departed loved one. I tried to dissuade them of this notion by telling them that no one, including me, was in charge of whether they saw a departed loved one. They themselves weren't even in charge. I just knew that some people experienced the presence of departed loved ones as result of this procedure and some did not. It has been that way for thousands of years, I told them.

To emphasize that I was no magician I took great care to tell new patients the history of gazing. I told them that in ancient Greece people had to wait twenty-nine days before they were permitted to gaze into the cauldron of water and find their departed loved one. Until that time, they had to wander around underground to put their mind "in the right place" to see the departed. Since then, many—including me—had reduced the amount of time for the entire procedure to approximately one day.

Still, many of the patients didn't really care about the history of the procedure. Many didn't even want to talk about their loved ones or reminisce about them through mementos. No, all they wanted to do was sit in the mirrored booth and wait for their loved ones to arrive. They had seen Oprah's producer do it, they had seen Joan Rivers do it, and they were sure they knew enough to do it themselves. The process meant nothing to them. They just wanted the instant gratification of going to the booth and seeing Grandma.

The expectations became too great for me. Although more than 80 percent of the people who came through the Theater of the Mind saw departed loved ones, 20 percent did not. I didn't like dealing with the disappointment of those who did not reach their goal.

I still have patients for my reunions work, but I have cut back greatly on the number of them. I tell patients up front about the process that needs to be followed, and I caution that if they aren't interested in performing every aspect of the process, then there is no need for them to even be there. I am also more careful in screening patients on the telephone. I ask them a series of questions that tell me in a matter of minutes whether they have the focus necessary to complete the reunions process successfully. Asking these questions doesn't ensure that every patient I accept will have contact with a loved one, but it has most assuredly increased the number of patients who leave with a smile on their face and a tear in their eye.

My reunions work has led me to soften the line that I believe exists between reality and the supernatural. I now feel that thoughts are things, and that reality is drawn not only from the supernatural *act* of thinking but also from the supernatural *way* of thinking. To realize how easy it is to evoke apparitions of the deceased was a major breakthrough, to my mind. To bring the world of the ancient Greeks into the modern world is an amazing act. Whether these techniques just access a place in our consciousness where memories of our deceased relative exist or actually extend our reach into the supernatural world is not the issue. On a human level, scrying is a successful treatment of the paralyzing psychological problem of grief. That is the point. Period.

When I think of my reunions work, I like to think of what Aristophanes said about humanity. Although what he said is over two thousand years old and Greek, it reads like an ageless Zen Buddhist koan and perfectly expresses the relationship for humans between body and spirit.

Humankind, fleet of life like tree leaves, unsubstantial as shadows, weak creatures of clay, wingless, ephemeral, sorrow worn, and dreamlike.

CHAPTER TWENTY-TWO

The subject of near-death experiences runs through both my professional and personal lives, keeping them joined and never letting me forget that while we are learning to live, we are also learning to die.

In 1992 my father passed away from multiple myeloma, a cancer that develops among the blood-producing cells in the bone marrow. I had such conflicted feelings about my father that I couldn't bear to be at his deathbed. As I looked back on our relationship, I realized it was both a blessing and a curse.

I feared my father greatly—I still do. He was not only a surgeon but a military officer in World War II—both professions that call for an overbearing and demanding personality. Being raised by a town full of loving women, I didn't take well to his lack of gentleness. And for that matter, he didn't take to my mildness. Regardless of the subject, he always took the position counter to my own. And he did so with a vengeance, voicing his disregard for my opinions in the most demeaning of ways.

I lived my life in constant fear of verbal and mental abuse, which made me the timid person I am. After his death, however, I could see a blessing in his dominance: He taught me about fallibility and the dangers of becoming too wedded to an opinion or position to be able to consider other options. I now realize that was one of the great positive messages I learned from his negative influence. Thanks to him, I became totally unconcerned about what the authorities think, just because they think it. Their opinions are worth hearing, but I still have to make up my own mind after weighing all of the evidence. And if the authorities don't like it, that doesn't deter me at all.

With the passage of time since his death, I have come to view my father as that fallible authority.

Because of this view of him I've developed over the years, I could perhaps bear to be at his deathbed if the situation were to present itself now. But in 1992, being with him at the hour of his death would have dredged up an intolerable amount of personal grief for me.

Nevertheless, what happened as he slipped away was a great vindication for my work. In the moments before his death, my brothers who were there at his side said his breathing picked up and they were amazed to see his eyes open; the doctors had told them he was in a coma from which he would not regain consciousness. He was wearing a beatific smile as he looked into their puzzled faces and said: "I have been to a beautiful place. Everything is okay. I'll see everybody again. I'll miss you, but we will be together again."

With that proclamation, he died.

Up until that point he had always felt dubious about my work in near-death experiences. He never fully embraced it and in fact thought it was foolish until I became famous for it and he himself achieved some personal notoriety for being the father of the *Life After Life* author. And we already know how he felt about my reunions work: The notion of seeing dead relatives was so crazy to him that he had me committed to a mental hospital.

I felt sad when I first heard about his last moments from my brothers, but then a sardonic thought intruded. Dad's deathbed experience made him a believer. If he had survived, he might well have been my next patient in the psychomanteum.

On May 8, 1994, Mother's Day, I called my mother in Macon, Georgia, from a pay phone at a shopping mall in Las Vegas, where I was attending a near-death studies conference at the University of Nevada, Las Vegas.

"Well, hello, Raymond," she said. "I knew you would call me today."

As a devout mama's boy, I found conversation with my mother to be a great comfort. This day was no different. I stood in the mall and enjoyed a long conversation with her. She told me all of the neighborhood gossip as well as what my brothers and sisters were doing. When I realized an hour had passed, I told her I had to get back to the conference.

"One more thing," I said before hanging up. "How are *you* doing?"

"Oh, I'm fine," she said. "Yesterday I got a rash on my arms, but Kay [my sister] took me to the emergency room and the doctor there said it was nothing. So I'm about as good as I can be."

I questioned her about the rash, but she downplayed it.

"All I know is it was driving me so crazy I had to go to emergency," she said. "The ER doctor got me an appointment with a dermatologist for tomorrow. We'll see what he says."

The next day my sister called me to report bad news. The rash was a late-stage symptom of non-Hodgkin's lymphoma, a fast-growing cancer of the white blood cells. Mom's was "fulminant"—the fastest-growing possible. According to the oncologist who analyzed her blood tests, she had perhaps no more than two weeks to live.

All of the siblings descended on Macon with the goal of making her final days as comfortable as possible. We cared for her at home, and when she was checked into the hospital we stayed at her bedside. Two weeks from the date of her diagnosis, she died.

It was in the final moments of her death that my next field of research was revealed.

She had been comatose for two days, so we didn't expect much to happen besides her quiet passing. Shortly before she died, however, she awoke and with great coherency told us that she loved us all very much.

"Please say that again," said my sister Kay.

With great effort, Mom pushed the oxygen mask from her face and said again, "I love you all very much."

We were deeply moved by her effort to express her love. We all held hands around the bed—my two sisters, their husbands, and Cheryl and I—and waited for the moment of death.

As we held hands the room seemed to change shape, and four of the six of us felt as though we were being lifted from the ground. I felt a strong pull like a riptide, only the pull was upward.

"Look," said my sister, pointing to a spot at the end of the bed. "Dad's here! He's come back to get her!"

Everyone later reported that the light in the room became soft and fuzzy, like looking into the water of a lighted swimming pool at night. Rather than sadness dominating the room, we all became joyful. As I wrote later, "It was as though the fabric of the universe had torn and for just a moment we felt the energy of that place called heaven."

My brother-in-law Rick Lanford, a Methodist minister, said that he felt as though he left his physical body and "went into another plane with her."

It was like nothing that had ever happened to any of us. Over the next several days we all spent hours together in my parents' home talking about the experience, trying to assemble all of the details into a coherent timeline. What had taken place with my mother was a shared-death experience. Shared-death experiences are like near-death experiences, but they happen, not to people who are dying, but to people who are in the proximity of a loved one who is dying. These spiritual experiences can happen to more than one person and are remarkably like near-death experiences.

I had heard of shared-death experiences before. The first time was from a Dr. Jamieson, who taught at the Medical College of Georgia and had been following my progress through near-death studies. One day she invited me to her office to talk about her own experience.

Jamieson had been visiting her mother two years earlier when her mom had a sudden cardiac arrest. Jamieson began CPR, performing chest compression and mouth-to-mouth for nearly thirty minutes before she realized that she was now an orphan.

Jamieson stopped, stunned by the situation she found herself in. Then, to her amazement, she found herself lifted out of her body and looking down on the CPR scene as though she were on a balcony. Trying to get her bearings, Jamieson looked to her left, and there was her mother, hovering with her. Then things got really strange. Jamieson looked in the corner of the room at what seemed to be a "breach in the universe," where light was pouring in. Within that light were people Jamieson had known for years; they were all friends of her mother's who had died.

Jamieson watched as her mother drifted into the light and into a reunion with her friends. Then the breach closed down in a spiral fashion like a camera lens and the light disappeared.

When it ended, she found herself next to her dead mother, totally puzzled about what had taken place in the seconds—or was it minutes?—before.

I didn't know what to make of Jamieson's story. This was early in my study of these phenomena, and I had never heard anyone recount an experience like this one. When she asked what I thought of it, I struggled for words, finally settling on a name for what had happened to her: "shared-death experience."

I didn't hear another such story until nearly ten years later, in the early eighties. That was the decade when everything opened up in medicine and doctors and nurses were no longer afraid to talk about the events taking place in hospitals that could be considered spiritual or paranormal. It was then that stories similar to Dr. Jamieson's came to me not only through physicians and nurses but also from the families of deceased patients.

I began to hear people talk about being with their dying loved one and seeing the room change shape and suddenly fill with a mystical light. There were stories about being swept into a tunnel of light with the person who was dying and seeing their life review. Sometimes several people would experience these events at the same time. It was as though the living were having near-death experiences.

Let me provide an excellent example of what I mean. This woman from upstate New York was at her mother's bedside when she died.

The first thing that happened when my mother passed was the Light changed intensity and grew much brighter real fast. All kinds of things started happening at once, such as a kind of rocking motion that went through my whole body. It was like my whole body rocked forward one time real quick, and then instantly I was seeing the room from a different angle from above and to the left side of the bed instead of the right side. It was like I was viewing my mother's body from the wrong side according to where I was stationed in the room.

This rocking-forward motion was very comfortable and not at all like a shudder, and especially not like when a car you are riding in lurches to the side and you get nauseous. I was not nauseous or feeling uncomfortable, but in fact the opposite where I felt far more comfortable and peaceful than I ever felt in my life.

I don't know whether I was out of my body or not, because all the other things that were going on held my attention. I was just glued to these scenes (from my mother's life) that were flashing throughout the room or around the bed. I cannot even tell whether the room was there anymore, or if it was, there was a whole section of it you hadn't noticed before. I would compare it to the surprise you would have if you had lived in the same house for many years but one day you opened up a closet and found a big secret compartment you didn't know about. This thing seemed so strange and yet perfectly natural at the same time.

The scenes that were flashing around in midair contained things that had happened to my mother, some of which I remembered but others I didn't. I could see her looking at the scenes too, and she sure recognized all of them though, as I could tell because of her expression as she watched. This all happened at once so there is no way of telling if that matches the situation.

The scenes of my mother's life reminded me of the old-fashioned flashbulbs going off. When they did, I saw some scenes of my mother's life in it like in one of the 3-D movies of the 1950s.

By the time the flashes of her life were going on, she was out of her body. I saw my father, who passed seven years before, standing there where the head of the bed would have been. By this point the bed was kind of irrelevant, and my father was coaching my mother out of her body.

That was amusing because in life he had been a football coach at the high school I attended. Frankly, I felt a little disappointed that he still had that coaching mentality, as if he had not moved on to better things since his death.

I looked right into his face, and a recognition of love passed between us, but he went right back to focusing on my mother. He looked like a young man, although he was seventy-nine when he died. There was a glow about him or all through him—very vibrant. He was full of life.

One of his favorite expressions was "Look alive!" and he sure did look alive when he was coaching my mother out of her body. A part of her that was transparent just stood right up, going through her body, and she and my father pranced off into this Light and disappeared.

The room sort of rocked again, or my body did, but this time backwards in the opposite direction, and then everything went back to normal.

I felt great tenderness from my mother and father. This entire event overflowed with love and kindness. Since that day I wonder: Is the world we live in just a figment of our imagination?

That was the very question I had when we had the experience with my mother: *Is the world we live in just a figment of our imagination?*

I found shared-death experience stories like this and others to be extremely valuable to the study of life after life. Skeptics have long said that near-death experiences are caused by a lack of oxygen to the brain as a person dies. This lack of oxygen causes people to hallucinate, they say, and near-death experiences are only dreams, the last gasp of a dysfunctional brain.

But shared-death experiences are different. They are extraordinary events that happen to people who are *not* ill but are most likely at the deathbed of a loved one. As that person dies the bystander has an extraordinary experience that mimics the near-death experience. Some parts of these experiences are subjective (for instance, people's claim that the room changed shape or that they saw a bright light that drew them toward it), while others are objective (as in witnessing a dying person's life review that reveals previously unknown secrets). And of course, sometimes groups of people experience mystical events.

After exploring the events surrounding the death of my mother, I decided that, yes, it was time to take a look at shared-death experiences.

CHAPTER TWENTY-THREE

ᔇ

With many questions in mind, I put together the case studies of shared-death experiences I had collected. Then I went out and collected more. I did this in a subtle way. During lectures about near-death experiences, I would describe the phenomenon of shared-death experiences.

"Shared-death experiences are like near-death experiences only they take place in people who aren't sick," I might say. "They might happen at the deathbed of a loved one, or they might take place elsewhere. Or they might happen to a group of people. But they resemble what we know as a near-death experience."

When I would ask whether anyone in the room had had such an experience, several people would hold up their hands. Later I would interview them in detail and in private.

Another source for shared-death experiences was the deathbed research of the Society for Psychical Research (SPR) in

England, from which I was able to gather nineteenth-century shared-death experiences. One of the books compiled by the pioneering researchers Edmund Gurney, Frederic Myers, and Frank Podmore, *Phantasms of the Living*, contains more than seven hundred cases of paranormal phenomena, many of them deathbed visions and shared-death experiences. Another book, *Death-Bed Visions: The Psychical Experiences of the Dying* by Sir William Barrett, a physics professor at the Royal College of Science in Dublin, is nothing less than the first scientific study of the minds of the dying. He concludes, by the way, that dying patients are often clear-thinking and rational and that the events around them are often spiritual and supernatural.

Typical of the shared-death experiences found in Barrett's book is this one:

> With reference to the incident I related to you, which happened several years ago, the following are the facts just as they occurred:
>
> I lost my daughter when she was seventeen years of age; she had been ill for some five years, and for eight months before her death had been confined to her bed. During all this time, and up to her death, she maintained a remarkable degree of intelligence and will. A fortnight before her death, one evening when I was leaning over the head of her bed, I asked her what she was thinking of, seeing her absorbed. She replied, "Little mother, look there," pointing to the bed-curtains. I followed the direction of her hand and saw a man's form, completely white, standing out quite clearly against the dark curtain. Having no ideas of spiritism, my emotion was intense, and I closed my eyes not wishing to see any longer. My child said to me, "You do not

reply." I had the weakness to declare to her, "I see nothing";
but my trembling voice betrayed me doubtless, for the child
added with an air of reproach, "Oh, little mother, I have
seen the same thing for the last three days at the same hour;
it's my dear father who has come to fetch me."

My child died 15 days later, but the apparition was not
repeated; perhaps it attained its greatest intensity on the
day I saw it.

(Signed) Z.G.

I studied shared-death experiences just as I had done with near-
death experiences nearly four decades earlier, dissecting them
into their elements. The shared-death experiences contained
most of the traditional elements of the near-death experience,
including tunnel experiences, seeing a bright mystical light, out-
of-body experiences, even the transformational quality found in
near-death experiencers. But there were four differences that I
found to be extraordinary and new.

Mystical Music: Those who have shared-death experiences very
often hear music emanating from the surroundings. It is common
for the music to be heard by several people, even those coming
and going, and it can frequently last for long periods of time. The
people I surveyed described this music in various ways. To some
it was "the most beautiful and intricate music I have ever heard,"
while to others it was "the soft, wild notes of an Aeolian harp."

This phenomenon was also reported in the nineteenth-
century work of researchers Gurney, Myers, and Podmore. There
is no known explanation, other than to call it "the music of the
spheres."

Geometric Changes in the Environment: Even though my family experienced this change in geometry when my mother died, it is still difficult for me to describe it, and the people I spoke to who had had the same experience were no better able to find words for it. A woman I interviewed said simply that the square room "shifted." A man who'd had a shared-death experience at the bedside of his mother offered a confusing description of a room that "collapsed and expanded at the same time. It was as though I was witnessing an alternative geometry." Others said that the room opened into an "alternative reality" where "time is not a factor." And still another person likened this change in geometry to Disneyland, in that "it made me realize that most of the stuff that happens in the world happens behind the scenes and that all we see is the surface, where the functioning part is."

I don't know what this change in geometry really means. From my personal experience and the descriptions of others, it seems as though people who are dying, and sometimes those around them, are led to a different dimension.

A Shared Mystical Light: The most profoundly transformative part of a near-death experience is the encounter with a mystical light. Those who see the light never forget it. Sometimes these individuals feel the light, as though it is palpable. Many NDEers declare that the light emits purity, love, and peace.

Those who have had shared-death experiences say the same thing. Individuals and groups have said that the room of a dying loved one "filled up" with light. Some describe this as "a light that is like being swept up into a cloud." I have heard it described as "a light that is vivid and bright, but not in the way that we see with our eyes." Other descriptors have been "translucent," "a light filled with love," "a light that tickled me," and a "long-lasting light that stays even when it's gone."

An experience of light shared by a number of people at a deathbed does a lot to demolish the skeptics' argument that the light seen by those who have near-death experiences is nothing more than the dying brain shorting out. If a number of people who are not ill or dying share a mystical experience of light, then the light can't be caused by the dying brain of just one of them.

Mist-ical Experience: Another common event in the shared-death experience is seeing emissions of mist from the dying. This mist is described as "white smoke," steam, fog, and so on. Often it takes on a human shape.

I have spoken to many doctors, nurses, and hospice workers who have seen this mist. One doctor in Georgia who saw it happen twice within six months said simply, "A mist formed over the chest area and hovered there." A hospice worker in North Carolina twice saw mist rising from a dying patient and described what she saw as clouds with "a sort of mist that forms around the head or chest. There seems to be some kind of electricity to it, like an electrical disturbance."

I don't know how to interpret the mist that some see at the point of death. There are so many who see it that it makes no sense to me to say that death is playing tricks on the eyes or that these are hallucinations. Plus, this is by far the most common element reported by those who have shared-death experiences.

Without question, the presence of a mist at death demands great attention. What is the composition of this mist? What does it look like *exactly?*

I am excited about doing further research in each one of these aspects of shared-death experiences, not least because these experiences tell us far more about the afterlife than do near-death experiences. Why? Because those who doubt a link between near-death experience and an afterlife feel that NDEs are nothing but hallucinations caused by fear or a lack of oxygen to the brain. They say it is a physiological phenomenon, not a spiritual one.

But people who have shared-death experiences are not ill. The fact that healthy people sitting at the bedside of a dying loved one have these experiences gives us an entirely new framework in which to discuss mankind's most perplexing question: what happens when we die?

It is through the study of shared-death experience that we may get a clearer answer to the question of what happens to our souls after death.

CONCLUSION

~

It is through the study of shared-death experience that we may get a clearer answer to the question of what happens to our souls after death.

That sentence is a big step forward for me. In the beginning, when I first named the near-death experience and started near-death studies, I made it a point to neither believe nor disbelieve in the existence of the soul or a place called heaven. I was raised in a family that didn't attend church or believe in God. But aside from that personal history, I felt it was unscientific to conclude that we have a soul or that there is an afterlife. To do so would mean to some people that I wasn't objective in my work, that all of my research was merely aimed at propping up a belief, not at testing one. My goal in this research was to remain a true skeptic in the ancient Greek sense—one who neither believes nor disbelieves but who keeps searching for truth.

After more than four decades of studying death and the possibility of an afterlife, I have come to realize that my opinion is buttressed by thousands of hours of research and deep logical thought of the type that few have devoted to this most important topic. I have concluded that if everyone else has an opinion on the subject of life after death, why shouldn't I? As a result of this conviction, I have become brazen about voicing my viewpoint.

One opportunity came when a documentary filmmaker interviewed me about the afterlife. With the cameras rolling, he asked me: "Why has it taken so long to answer the question, 'Is there an afterlife?'"

"It's no surprise that the biggest and most important question of existence would defy our best and most rational means of solving it," I said. "The question is so unfathomable in a way because by definition death means 'the state from which you don't get back.' So we are dealing here with an enormously complex question, and it would be scholarly misconduct for somebody to portray this as an easy question that is going to yield with little effort."

"But it's obviously frustrating," he said. "No one has been able to answer the question of an afterlife. It's almost incomprehensible, unfathomable, really."

"The notion of eternity *is* unfathomable," I said. "But that doesn't deter me as a lover of philosophy from thinking about it. This physical realm in which we live is unfathomable too. If you don't think so, ask yourself basic questions about the size of the universe, or even how we got here, and you quickly get into unfathomable realms of thought, just like you do when addressing the spiritual realm. I'm okay with that. Part of the excitement of life is that we get to ponder things we don't understand. If I knew everything and there was nothing left to explore, that would be ghastly to me, boring. I am glad that there is no state in which we know everything."

"So what do you think happens when we die?" he asked.

My mind flashed back to the thousands of people I have listened to over the years as they told their story of near-death and the miraculous journey they took at the moment they almost died. I thought about my own journey to the brink of death. I realized that, yes, I was very experienced in both objective *and* subjective research into life after death. I answered the question from the heart.

"What do I think happens when we die? I think we enter into another state of existence or another state of consciousness that is so extraordinarily different from the reality we have here in the physical world that the language we have is not yet adequate to describe this other state of existence or consciousness. Based on what I have heard from thousands of people, we enter into a realm of joy, light, peace, and love in which we discover that the process of knowledge does not stop when we die. Instead, the process of learning and development goes on for eternity."

"That's quite a concept," he said. "How does this make you feel about God and his intentions?"

"I feel good about God," I said. "I have a relationship with God and talk to him all the time. But what I really don't know, from a rational point of view, is whether life after death is in his plan or not. And it may well be that God has something in mind for us that is even more remarkable than a life after death, which means the terminology we use in this frame of reference may not be adequate. There may even be a subsequent state of existence in which the notion of an afterlife as we know it is invalid. I love

God, I have a trusting relationship with him, but he hasn't told me anything yet about an afterlife."

Until he does, I am going to keep searching for answers. The spiritual universe is a very big place, and the joy of exploration I find in it is boundless.

ABOUT THE AUTHORS

Raymond Moody, MD, PhD, is the bestselling author of twelve books which have sold over 20 million copies. His seminal work, *Life After Life,* has completely changed the way we view death and dying and has sold over 13 million copies worldwide. Called "the father of the near-death experience" by the *New York Times,* Dr. Moody has researched a variety of paranormal experiences, from ghost sightings to past lives. Dr. Moody received his medical degree from the College of Georgia and his PhD in philosophy from the University of Virginia, where he also received his MA and BA For more information visit his website: www.lifeafterlife.com.

Paul Perry has co-written four *New York Times* bestsellers, including *Evidence of the Afterlife* (HarperOne), with Dr. Jeffrey Long. Perry is also a documentary filmmaker whose work has appeared internationally on television. This is the fifth book he has written with Dr. Moody. For more information, visit his website: www .paulperryproductions.com.